Easy Access
for Windows

Jeffry L. Byrne

Easy Access™ 2 for Windows™

Copyright © 1994 by Que® Corporation.

Library of Congress Catalog No.: 94-65524

ISBN: 1-56529-714-8

96 95   6   5   4   3   2

Interpretation of the printing code: the rightmost double-digit number is the year of the book's printing; the rightmost single-digit number, the number of the book's printing. For example, a printing code of 94-1 shows that the first printing of the book occurred in 1994.

Screen reproductions in this book were created with Collage Complete from Inner Media, Inc., Hollis, NH.

Publisher: David P. Ewing

Associate Publisher: Michael Miller

Publishing Director: Don Roche, Jr.

Managing Editor: Michael Cunningham

Product Marketing Manager: Ray Robinson

Credits

Acquisitions Editor
Nancy Stevenson

Product Directors
Steven M. Schafer
Joyce J. Nielsen

Production Editor
Michael Cunningham

Editors
Linda Seifert
Kathy Simpson

Technical Editor
Cathy Parkerson

Book Designer
Amy Peppler-Adams

Cover Designer
Dan Armstrong

Production Team
Steve Adams
Angela Bannan
Claudia Bell
Teresa Forrester
Joelynn Gifford
Bob LaRoche
Elizabeth Lewis
Tim Montgomery
Wendy Ott
Nanci Sears Perry
Linda Quigley
Dennis Sheehan
Amy L. Steed
Michael Thomas
Sue VandeWalle
Mary Beth Wakefield
Lillian Yates

Indexer
Michael Hughes

Composed in *Stone Serif* and *MCPdigital* by Que Corporation

About the Author

Jeffry Byrne lives in Portland, Oregon, with his wife Marisa, three dogs, and two cats. Jeff is the author of Que's *Paradox 4 QuickStart*, *Using CA-Simply Money*, and coauthor of *Using Quickbooks for Windows* and *Using PowerPoint*. He has also written other books on popular spreadsheet programs and documentation for database and point-of-sale programs. In his spare time, Jeff works as the purchasing manager for a local computer retailer and network installation house.

Acknowledgments

I would like to thank both Nancy Stevenson for helping me begin this project, and Tom Godfrey for helping me finish it, as well as all the other Que people who put many long hours into *Easy Access 2 for Windows*.

Trademarks

All terms mentioned in this book that are known to be trademarks or service marks have been appropriately capitalized. Que Corporation cannot attest to the accuracy of this information. Use of a term in this book should not be regarded as affecting the validity of any trademark or service mark.

Contents at a Glance

Contents

Part IV: Using Database Forms — 98

Part V: Getting Information from a Database — 140

Part VI: Creating and Using Reports   170

Part VII: Managing Database Files   192

Part VIII: Sample Documents   212

Part IX: Glossary   222

Index   228

Introduction

Introduction

What You Can Do with Access

Microsoft Access for Windows is one of the world's most popular database programs for the Windows environment. You can quickly and easily use this program to accomplish many database management tasks. For example, you can use Access for Windows to track the following types of information:

■ List of customer contacts

■ Personal address and phone list

■ Mailing lists and labels

■ Sales reports

■ Sales order database

■ Inventory control

Each of these familiar items is a type of database or report. Everyday you work with many databases; your personal phone book, a customer list, a product catalog, or an employee record are all forms of a database. A computerized database, such as Access for Windows, has several advantages over a paper database, including the following:

■ *You can quickly and easily change information contained in the database.* If a supplier's address changes, you simply have to edit the address in the supplier's database. The new address will then be reflected on your purchase orders and accounts payable.

■ *You can choose selected records from your database that meet criteria that you specify.* For example, instead of searching through your files for all your customers who bought green widgets last year, you can query Access for Windows to search for you.

■ *With Access for Windows, you can examine the information in your database and create many different reports.* For example, you can create reports that will show you all accounts that are more than 30 days past-due, or one that shows all your customers who have spent more than $1,000 in your store in the last year.

CommonName	FlowerColor	NumberPlanted
FLEABANE AZURE BEAUTY	BLUE	
BUXTON'S BLUE	BLUE	56
PRITCHARD'S BLUE	BLUE	12
OX-EYE CHAMOMILE	BLUE	8
	BLUE	10

■ *You can analyze and display the information contained in your database in different formats.* Using the same database, you can create mailing labels, phone lists, customer order summaries, and inventory on-hand reports by using your information in different ways.

You can use Access for Windows to create and maintain many different types of databases. Whether you want to keep track of your personal household assets or a complete set of database tables to keep track of your business's customers, inventory, payables, and receivables, Access for Windows can easily fit your information needs.

Task Layout

Easy Access for Windows is designed with you, the beginner, in mind. It has been divided into several parts. Each part contains several tasks that are related to each other.

In Part I, "Learning the Basics," you will learn general information about using Access for Windows.

In Part II, "Creating a Database Table," you will learn how to create an Access for Windows database file and table.

In Part III, "Entering and Editing Data," you learn how to enter and change information in your database table.

In Part IV, "Using Database Forms," you will learn to create and then use a form.

In Part V, "Getting Information from a Database," you will learn how to ask questions about the information in your table.

In Part VI, "Creating and Using Reports," you will learn to create and then print or display a report.

In Part VII, "Managing Database Files," you will learn to copy, rename, and delete database files.

In Part VIII, "Sample Documents," you can view some of the documents that can be created with Access for Windows.

Finally, Part IX is a glossary of frequently used terms in Microsoft Access for Windows.

Introduction

Task Sections

The Task sections include numbered steps that tell you how to accomplish certain tasks such as saving a workbook or filling a range. The numbered steps walk you through a specific example so that you can learn the task by doing it.

Big Screen

At the beginning of each task is a large screen that shows how the computer screen will look after you complete the procedure that follows in that task. Sometimes the screen shows a feature discussed in that task, however, such as a shortcut menu.

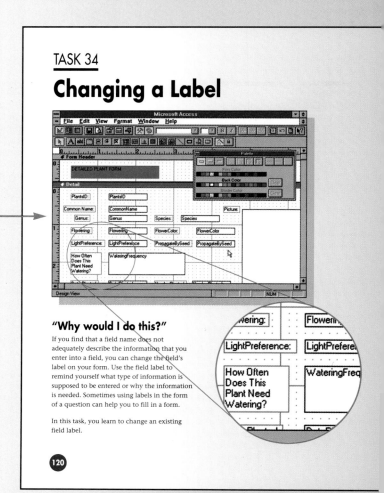

TASK 34

Changing a Label

"Why would I do this?"

If you find that a field name does not adequately describe the information that you enter into a field, you can change the field's label on your form. Use the field label to remind yourself what type of information is supposed to be entered or why the information is needed. Sometimes using labels in the form of a question can help you to fill in a form.

In this task, you learn to change an existing field label.

120

Why Worry? Notes

You may find that you performed a task, such as sorting data, that you didn't want to do after all. The Why Worry notes tell you how to undo certain procedures or get out of a situation such as displaying a Help screen.

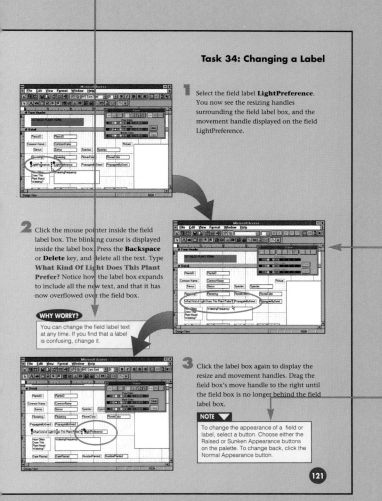

Task 34: Changing a Label

1 Select the field label **LightPreference**. You now see the resizing handles surrounding the field label box, and the movement handle displayed on the field LightPreference.

2 Click the mouse pointer inside the field label box. The blinking cursor is displayed inside the label box. Press the **Backspace** or **Delete** key, and delete all the text. Type **What Kind Of Light Does This Plant Prefer?** Notice how the label box expands to include all the new text, and that it has now overflowed over the field box.

WHY WORRY?
You can change the field label text at any time. If you find that a label is confusing, change it.

3 Click the label box again to display the resize and movement handles. Drag the field box's move handle to the right until the field box is no longer behind the field label box.

NOTE
To change the appearance of a field or label, select a button. Choose either the Raised or Sunken Appearance buttons on the palette. To change back, click the Normal Appearance button.

121

Step-by-Step Screens

Each task includes a screen shot for each step of a procedure that shows how the computer screen will look at each step in the process.

Other Notes

Many tasks contain other short notes that tell you a little more about certain procedures. These notes define terms, explain other options, refer you to other sections when applicable, and so on.

7

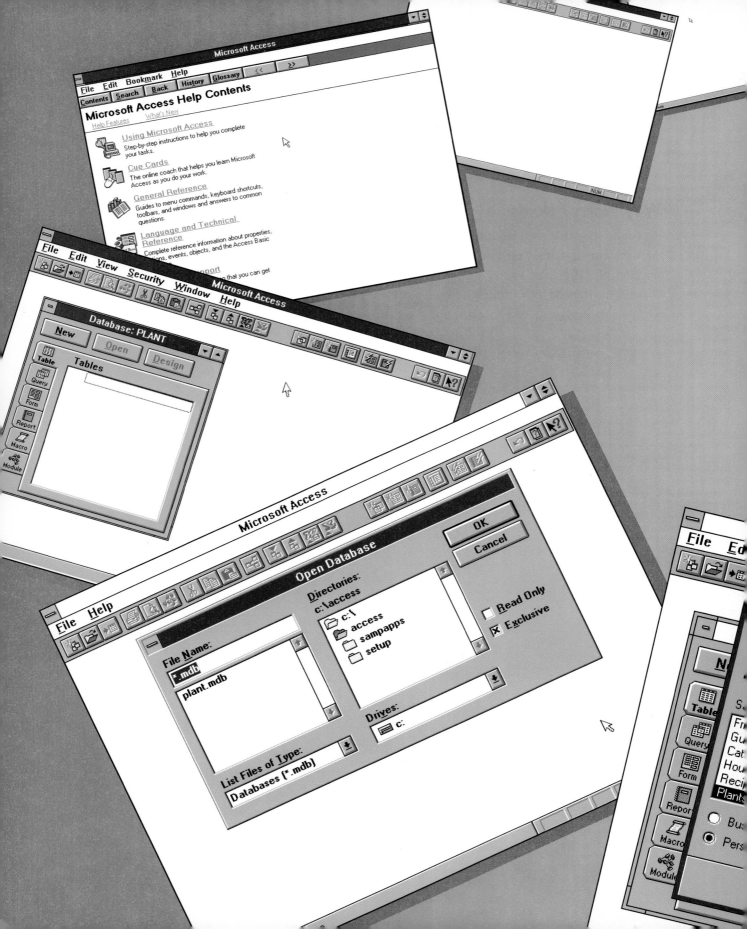

PART I
Learning the Basics

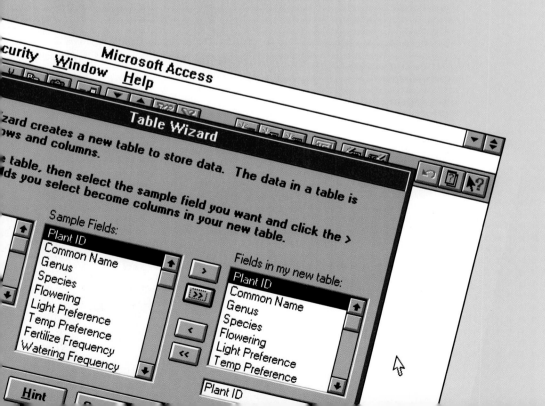

Part I: Learning the Basics

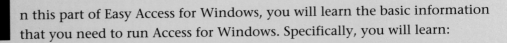

I n this part of Easy Access for Windows, you will learn the basic information that you need to run Access for Windows. Specifically, you will learn:

■ What an Access for Windows database is

■ How to use a mouse with Access for Windows

■ How to use your keyboard with Access for Windows

■ How to use the Access for Windows Desktop Window

■ How to select a menu command

■ How to select a Toolbar button

■ How to use Cue Cards and get help

■ How to start and exit Access for Windows

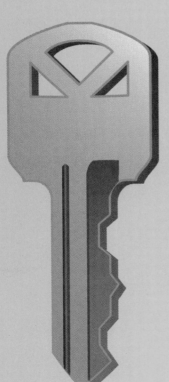

Before you continue much further with *Easy Access for Windows*, you should be familiar with a few simple database concepts. A database such as Access for Windows is organized into one or more *tables*. A table of information is arranged in *rows* and *columns*.

Each row of the table is called a *record*. The record consists of all the information about a single entry in the table. A record may be a customer's name, address, telephone number, credit limit, and customer number.

Each column of the table is called a *field*. A field is the smallest distinct piece of information contained in a record. You may have individual fields for a customer's last name, first name, street address, city, state, and ZIP code.

You can create a database composed of several tables that are each related in some way. Each table holds a specific part of the database. One table may contain information about customers, another about invoice information, and a third about products. Tables can be combined or joined to form a working database.

In this part of *Easy Access for Windows*, you will learn how to open Access for Windows and create a database field. If you are already familiar with using Windows and are comfortable with opening and exiting from programs, you may want to skip to Task 3. If you are completely new to using Windows, please be sure to read through this part and try each of the tasks before you continue.

Although you can access most of the features of Access for Windows using either the mouse or keyboard, you will use your keyboard to enter most of the information into a table.

Starting Access for Windows

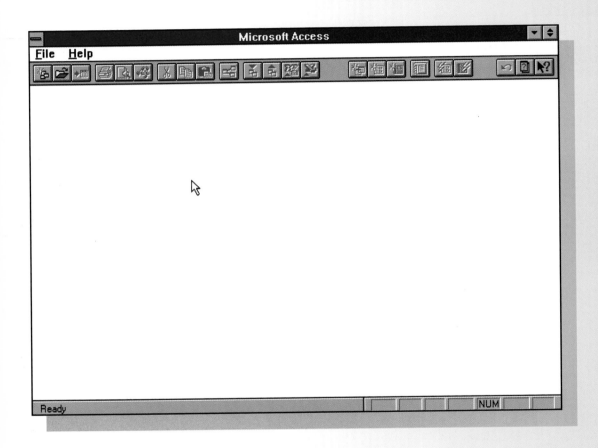

"Why would I do this?"

Before you can work in Access for Windows, you must first start the program. Access for Windows is a database program that operates only within the Windows environment.

In this task, you will learn to start Windows, and then start Access for Windows.

C:\>WIN

1 Type **WIN** and press the **Enter** key. This command will load Windows into your computer's memory.

2 Double-click the Microsoft Office group icon. Then double-click the Microsoft Access 2.0 program icon.

NOTE ▼

Windows stores all programs in program group windows on the Program Manager desktop. If the Microsoft Access group window is open—as are the program groups Main and Accessories—you can skip this step and go directly to step 3.

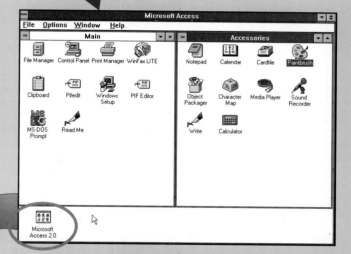

3 Your computer will now load Access for Windows into your computer's memory.

WHY WORRY?

If Access for Windows does not begin to open when you double-click, try again. You may need to click the mouse more rapidly or more squarely on the icon.

Choosing Menu Commands and Toolbar Buttons

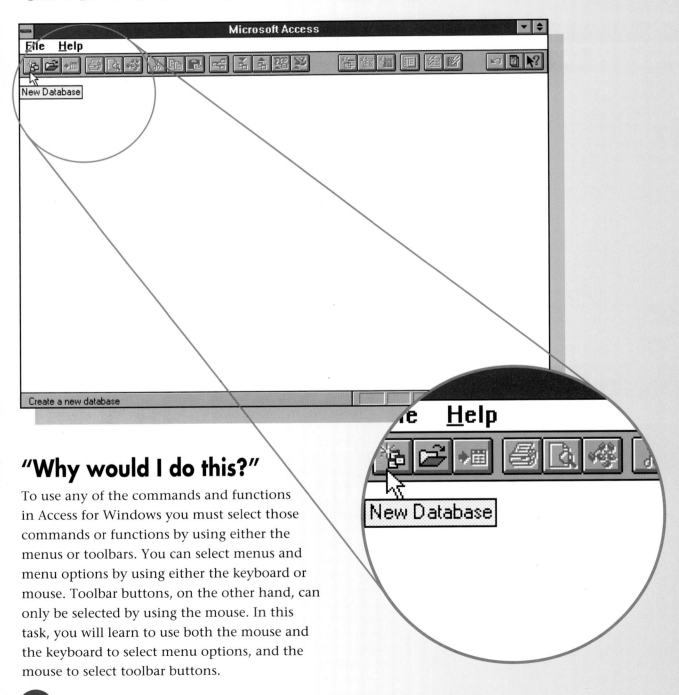

"Why would I do this?"

To use any of the commands and functions in Access for Windows you must select those commands or functions by using either the menus or toolbars. You can select menus and menu options by using either the keyboard or mouse. Toolbar buttons, on the other hand, can only be selected by using the mouse. In this task, you will learn to use both the mouse and the keyboard to select menu options, and the mouse to select toolbar buttons.

Task 2: Choosing Menu Commands and Toolbar Buttons

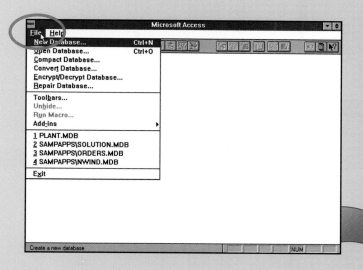

1 Move the mouse pointer to the menu option **File** and click the left mouse button once. You have opened the File drop-down menu. Press the **Esc** key to remove the drop-down menu from view.

NOTE ▼

Moving the mouse pointer anywhere outside of the drop-down menu and clicking once will also remove the menu.

2 Press and hold the **Alt** key on your keyboard, then press the **F** key. You again see the File drop-down menu list. An underlined letter in a menu command or option is called a *hot key*. To use the hot key, press and hold the Alt key, then press the underlined letter.

NOTE ▼

To choose a menu from the keyboard, hold down the Alt key and press the underlined letter in the name of the menu. To choose an item from the drop-down menu, type the underlined letter of that option.

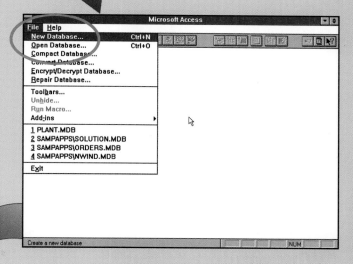

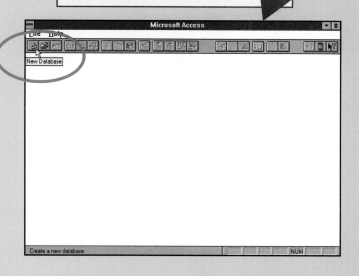

3 Move the mouse pointer to the first button on the toolbar. You will see the button description displayed underneath the mouse pointer. Click the left mouse button once to activate the function for that toolbar button. All toolbar buttons are used this way.

Getting Help

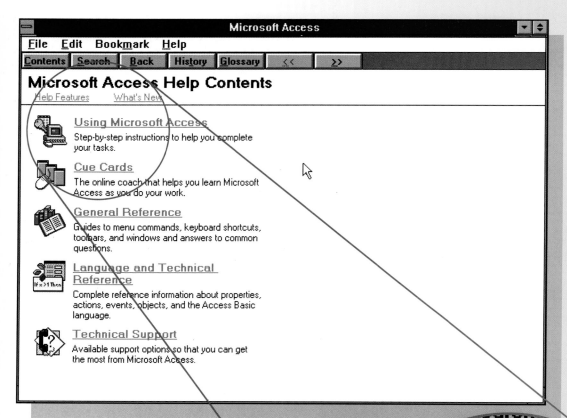

"Why would I do this?"

There will be times, probably more than once, when you will need help with Access for Windows. Access for Windows provides you with several avenues for getting help. There is always the documentation provided with the program, but you can also access on-line help. You can search for a specific command or procedure, access context-sensitive help, or view the Cue Cards.

In this task, you will learn to access each of the different on-line help options available to you.

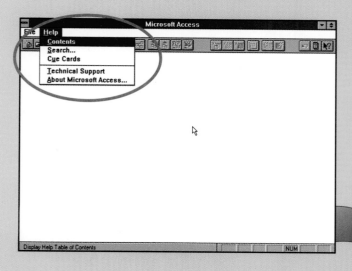

1 Click the **Help** command on the menu bar. This will display the drop-down menu showing the list of help options.

2 Click the first option, **Contents**. You will see the Microsoft Access Help Contents window. From this window you can access any of the other on-line help screens.

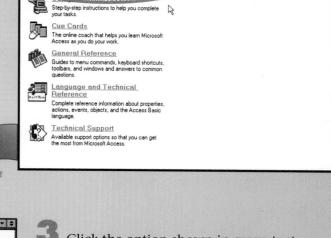

NOTE ▼

Moving the mouse pointer to any text displayed in green will cause the pointer to change shape to a small hand with a pointing index finger. By clicking the mouse at these points, you can display additional help screens or definition boxes.

3 Click the option shown in green text **Using Microsoft Access**. From this window you can access help for many different topics. Remember, use the scroll bar to display additional help topics that are not currently visible on this screen.

Task 3: Getting Help

4 Click the **Back** button on the Help windows button bar. This will return you to the previous window. Click the option shown in green text, **Cue Cards**.

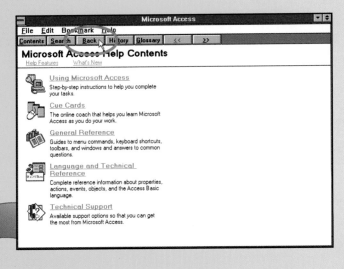

5 The Access for Windows Cue Cards can be used for a quick overview of the program, or you can use them to coach you through some of the more common Access for Windows tasks. Click the > button beside the See a quick overview option.

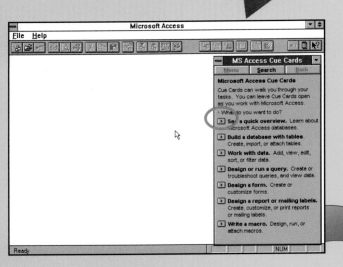

6 Click the > button beside the See a quick overview option. This will access the next level of Cue Cards.

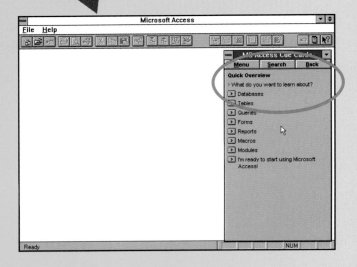

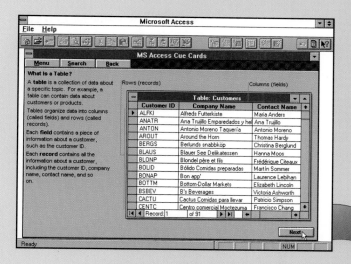

7 Click the > button beside the Tables option. This command will open the next Cue Cards in the series.

WHY WORRY?

You can use the Back button on the button bar to return to the previous Cue Card. If you are ready to see the next Cue Card in a series, press the Next button in the lower-right corner of the screen.

8 Click the **Control menu** button in the upper left corner of the Cue Card dialog box. This will display the Control menu for the Cue Card dialog box.

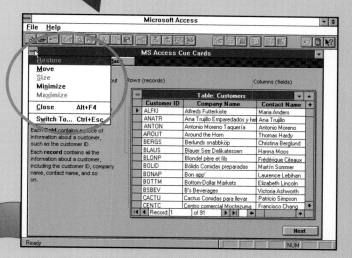

9 Select the **Close** command from the Control menu. You will now be returned to the Access for Windows desktop.

NOTE ▼

Remember, you can also press key combination Alt+F4 to close the dialog box.

Task 3: Getting Help

10 Click the **Help** button on the toolbar. This button is the last button on the toolbar, and it enables you to get context-sensitive help on any procedure that you are working on. The mouse pointer will change shape to an arrow with a question mark.

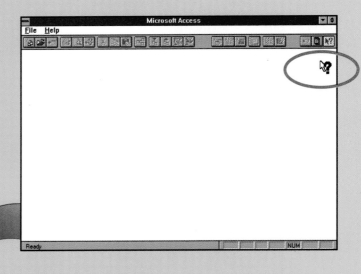

11 Move the mouse pointer to the object that you want to get help with, then click. The illustration shown here is the Help screen displayed by clicking on the toolbar.

NOTE ▼

You also can receive help from Access for Windows at any time by pressing the F1 key. Access for Windows will display the appropriate Help screen for the procedure or object that you are working with.

12 Click **File** from the Help window menu. This will display the File drop-down menu showing the list of File commands. Click **Exit** from the drop-down menu to return to the Access for Windows desktop.

WHY WORRY?

For almost any problem, Access can provide an answer for you. With just a click of the mouse or a few keystrokes, you can display a Help screen.

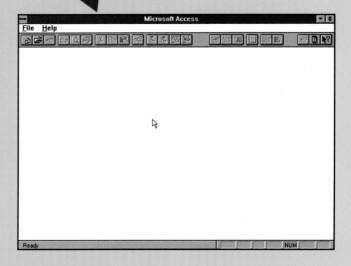

Exiting Access for Windows

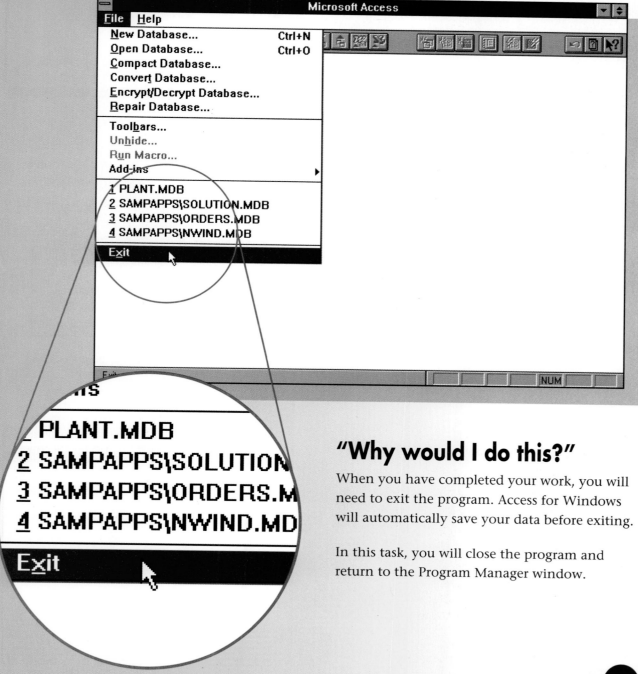

"Why would I do this?"

When you have completed your work, you will need to exit the program. Access for Windows will automatically save your data before exiting.

In this task, you will close the program and return to the Program Manager window.

Task 4: Exiting Access for Windows

1 Click **File** on the menu bar. This step will display the drop-down menu showing the list of File commands. Click **Exit**.

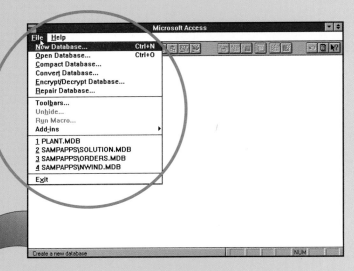

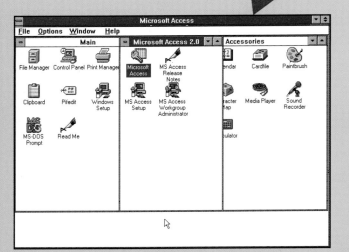

2 This step will close Access for Windows and return you to the Windows Program Manager.

NOTE ▼

You can accomplish this same task by pressing the Alt+F4 key combination. When pressed, this key combination will universally exit from a window, a program, or from Windows itself.

WHY WORRY?

If you have inadvertently selected the File command and are not yet ready to exit from Access for Windows, press the Esc key. This will close the menu. You can also click the mouse anywhere on the Access for Windows desktop—outside the menu list—to close the menu.

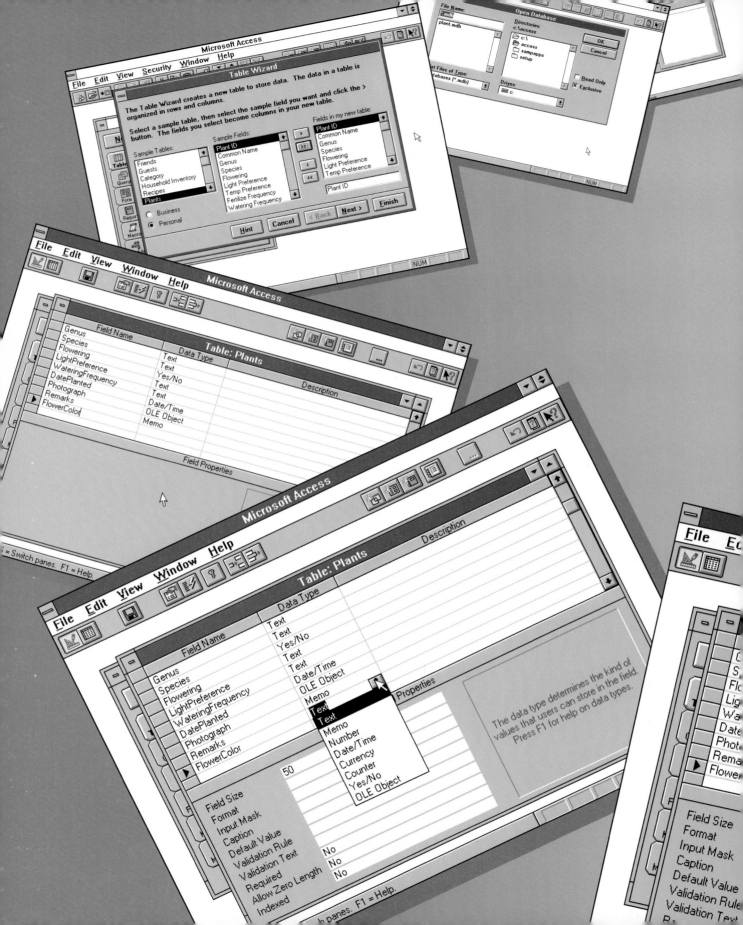

PART II

Creating a Database Table

25

Part II: Creating a Database Table

Access for Windows is a database that stores information or data in a table format. Once the information is in the database, you can ask Access to retrieve the information to your screen or print it out in reports.

An Access for Windows table can hold any information that you require. For example, you could create a table that contains all the information related to your customers and their orders. The table holds pieces of information in fields such as: Customer Name, Address, Invoice #, Invoice Date, Item Sold, Quantity Sold, and Price.

Depending on your type of business, you might need to add other fields such as Phone Number and Fax number. As your table grows, it could become hard to handle. Also, as you enter information for a repeat customer, you will frequently be repeating the same customer information. The table would quickly grow, requiring more and more precious disk space, and become harder to search through because of so much duplicated information.

The idea being a database is to remove the need to duplicate information. A table is created to hold a specific type of information. If for some reason you need to edit data, for example a customer's address, you would only have to perform this task in one place—not for each line that the customer's address occurs on. A database used to track the same information shown above could include the following:

Customer	Invoice	Inventory
Customer ID	Invoice #	Item Code
Customer Name	Item Code	Item
Description	Quantity	Item Cost
Address	Item Cost	
Invoice #		

Each of these tables contains information that is unique to that table and a field that provides a link to at least one other table.

Each row of a table is an individual *record*. Each record is made up of the fields that describe the table subject. In the case of the Customer table, each record holds all the information about a single customer.

Each piece of information for a record is in an element called a *field*. In the case of the Customer table there are fields for: Customer ID, Customer Name, and Address.

You can format a field to control the type of data that it contains. For example, you can format the Quantity field to accept only numbers. This would prevent you from accidentally entering *ABC* into this field. You also can format a field to accept dates or text of a specified length.

In this part, you are introduced to the essential elements that go into creating a table.

Creating a New Database File

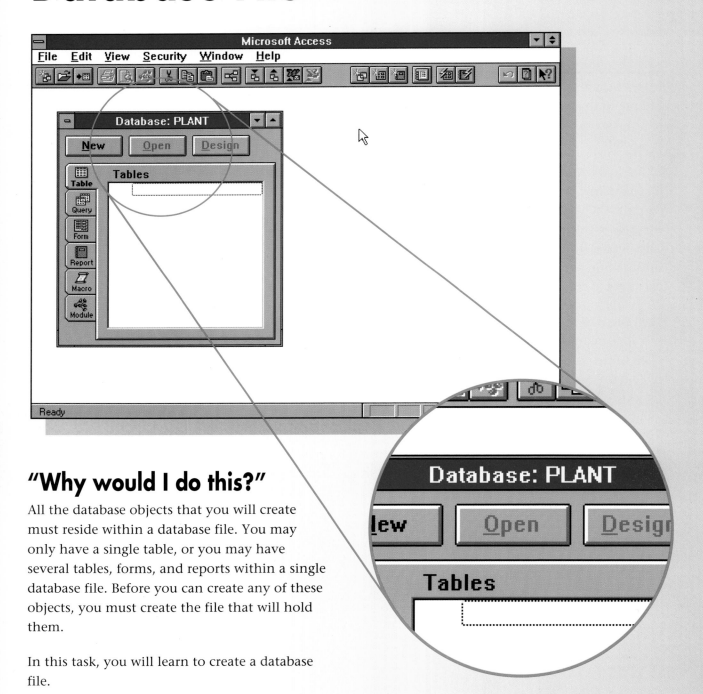

"Why would I do this?"

All the database objects that you will create must reside within a database file. You may only have a single table, or you may have several tables, forms, and reports within a single database file. Before you can create any of these objects, you must create the file that will hold them.

In this task, you will learn to create a database file.

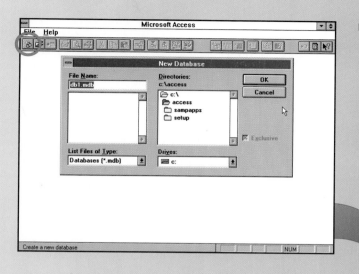

1 Click the **New Database** button on the toolbar, which is located at the far left side of the toolbar. Access for Windows automatically names a database. The default name for your first database file is DB1.MBD. Subsequent databases are named DB2.MBD, DB3.MBD, and so on. Unless you plan to only use a single database, give your database a more descriptive name.

2 Type **plant** and press the **Enter** key. Access for Windows will automatically add the file extension .MBD for you and create the database file. By giving your database a more descriptive file name, you will be able to easily see what each database file is for. By letting Access for Windows use the default file names DB1.MBD, DB2.MBD, and so on, you may have to open and close several database files to find the one that you want to work in—unless you keep a written list of each file.

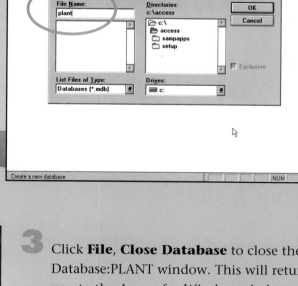

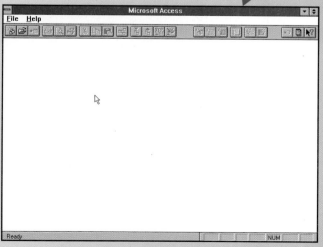

3 Click **File**, **Close Database** to close the Database:PLANT window. This will return you to the Access for Windows desktop.

 NOTE

You also can click File, New Database to open the New Database dialog box, or use the keyboard shortcut Ctrl+N.

TASK 6

Opening a Database

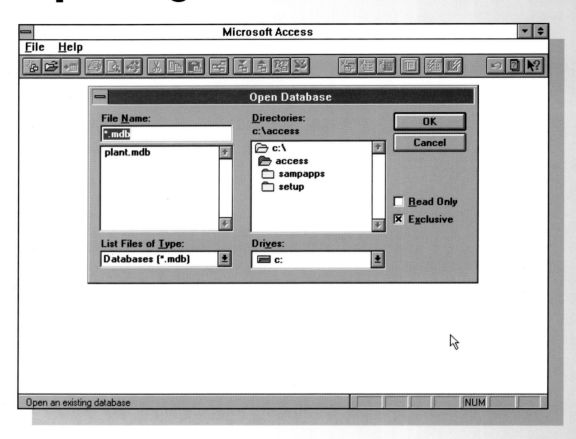

"Why would I do this?"

To use a database file, you must open it first. By opening the database file, you gain access to the database tables, forms, and other objects.

In this task, you will learn how to open an existing database file.

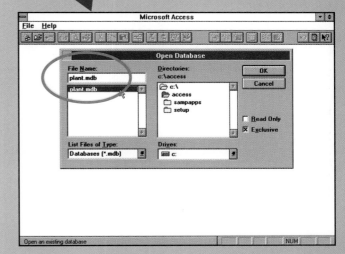

1 Click the **Open Database** button on the toolbar. This will display the Open Database dialog box.

NOTE ▼

You also can access the Open Database dialog box by clicking File, Open Database from the menu bar, or by using the keyboard shortcut Ctrl+O.

2 Click the name of the database that you want to use, and then click **OK**. Database file names are displayed in the scrolling list box displayed beneath the text box labeled File Name. If necessary, use the scroll bar to view file names that are not displayed.

NOTE ▼

You also can type the name of the database file in the File Name text box, and then press Enter. You also can double-click the file name in the list box.

WHY WORRY?

If you select the wrong database file, close it and open the correct file.

Creating a New Database Table

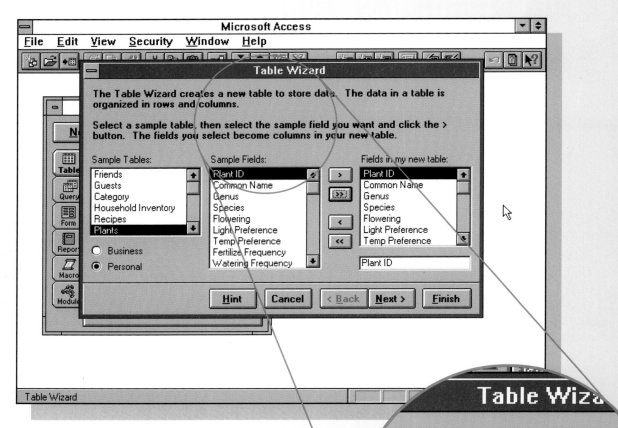

"Why would I do this?"

Before you can complete other tasks, you must first create your database table. A database is built on one or more tables that each hold a specific type of information.

In the following task, you will create a new database table using the Table window in Design view. You will use Design view in the next several tasks to define your table.

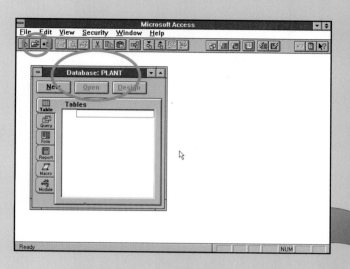

1 Open the database file to which you want to add a table by clicking the **Open Database** button on the toolbar, and then double-clicking the name of the file to be opened. For this task, open the database PLANT.

NOTE ▼

The Database window will display a listing of all tables that are available in the list box. Because this is the first table to be created, the list box is empty.

2 Click the **New** button. The New Table dialog box is displayed. From here, you can create a table from scratch by clicking the **New Table** button, or you can use the Table Wizards. The Table Wizards can provide you with invaluable help and many predesigned tables.

NOTE ▼

You also can press Alt+N to activate the New button, or press Enter.

3 Click the **Table Wizards** button in the New Table dialog box. The Access Table Wizard can help you set up a complete or partial database table. You can choose from 26 Business category and 19 Personal category tables. Using these predefined tables can save you a great deal of time.

Task 7: Creating a New Database Table

4 Click the radio button labeled **Personal**. Access for Windows will display the Personal category list of tables.

NOTE ▼

To view other types of available tables, scroll up and down both the Business and Personal lists.

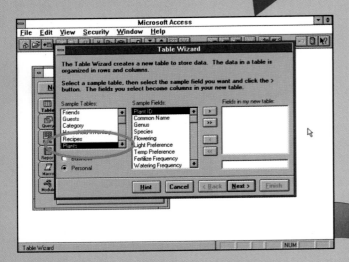

5 Scroll down the Sample Tables list box until you see the table name Plants; click once to select it. You will see a new list displayed in the Sample Fields list box.

6 Select the **Common Name** field from the Sample Fields list box to be included in your own table. Highlight a field by clicking it. The field is then selected.

NOTE ▼

When you select and add a field from the Sample Fields list to your own list, you add the field name and all the formatting information of the selected field. You learn to edit this information later in this part.

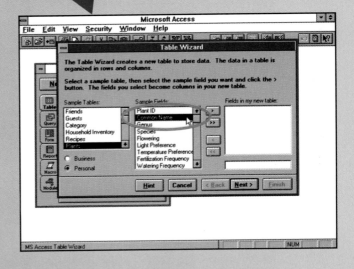

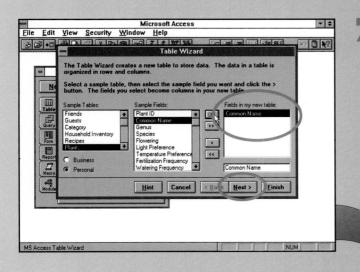

7 Click the **Next >** button. You will see the field name copied to the Fields in my new table list box. Repeat steps 6 and 7 for each field that you want to have included in your new table. If you are not sure about a field, go ahead and include it. You can easily delete a field later if you find that you do not use it. Add these additional fields to your own list box: Genus, Species, Flowering, Light Preference, Watering Frequency, Date Planted, Photograph, and Note.

8 Change the name of the selected field Note in the lower right-hand corner of the Wizard window. After selecting the word, type the new name **Remarks** in the text box. Notice how the selected field Note from the Sample Fields list has been renamed Remarks in your list box. You can rename any of your new fields in this manner without changing any of the formatting characteristics of the field. Select the **Next >** button.

9 You will now see the next Table Wizard dialog box. Use this dialog box to enter a name for your table, or to select a primary key for your table. If you want to change the table name from the default name, type a new name into the text box. Select the **Next >** button.

Task 7: Creating a New Database Table

10 The final Table Wizard dialog box appears; use it to decide where you will go next. Choose **Modify the table design** radio button to go to the Table Design view. The second radio button opens your new table so you can begin to enter data. The third radio button enables you to enter data using a form instead of typing it directly into the table. You can display Cue Cards by clicking the check box.

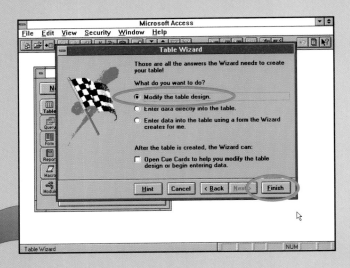

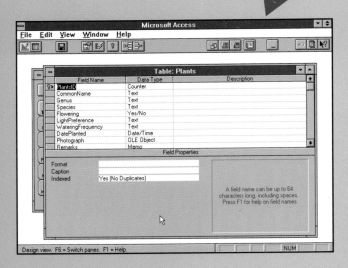

11 Click the **Finish** button. Access for Windows will display your table in the Table Design view window.

WHY WORRY?

You can edit your table design at any time. Select the table from the list in the Database window and click the Design button.

Entering a New Field

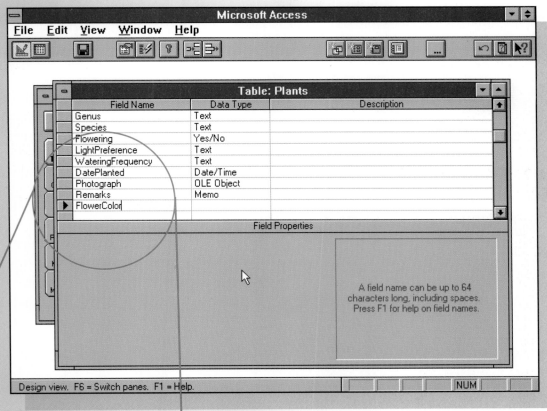

"Why would I do this?"

At any time that you add fields to a table, you must name the field. A field name should describe the contents of the information contained in the field.

In this task, you will learn how to create a field name.

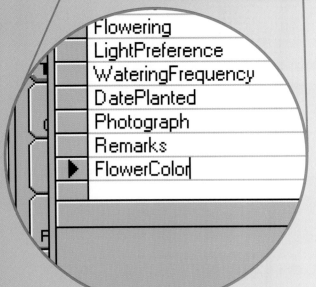

Task 8: Entering a New Field

1 Press the **down-arrow** key until you come to the first blank row. You will enter your new field name into this row, in the Field Name column.

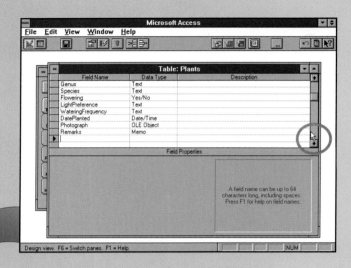

2 Type **FlowerColor** in the Field Name column and press **Enter**. You can create a field name with a maximum of 64 characters. You can use any combination of letters, numbers, spaces, and characters. The exceptions include: periods (.), exclamation points (!), single quote marks ('), brackets ([or]), and spaces at the beginning of the field name.

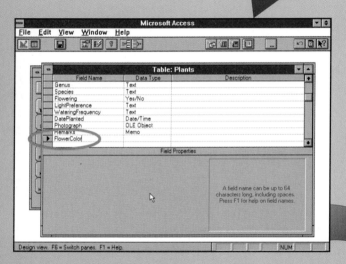

3 Click the **arrow** button that is shown in the Data Type field. This will display the drop-down list of available Data Type options. You must select one of these options. Access for Windows will enter the default option, Text, if you do not make another selection. Because Access for Windows enters Text as the default data type and text is the required data type for this field, this step is optional.

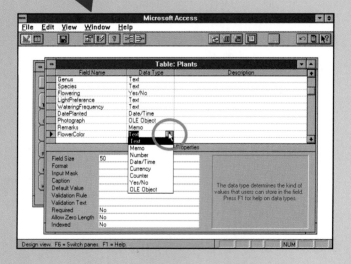

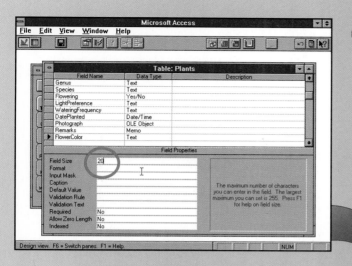

4 Press **F6**, to select the Field Size text box, and type **20**. The Field Size property enables you to specify the length of the field. (The maximum length for a text field is 255 characters; the default setting is 50 characters.) After you type a number for the field size, press the **down-arrow** key to move to the next property. To accept the default setting, press the **down-arrow** key.

5 Press the **F6** key, or click the mouse on the line in the Description column for the field to which you want to add the descriptive line.

NOTE ▼

Do not arbitrarily set a text field to 255 characters. If you set a large number for the field size, Access for Windows uses that number to allocate memory and disk storage requirements—even if you only enter a few characters. You can easily increase a field's size to meet your needs.

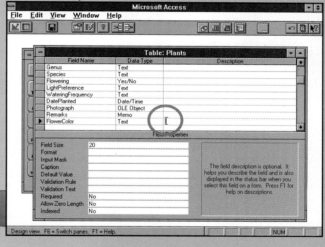

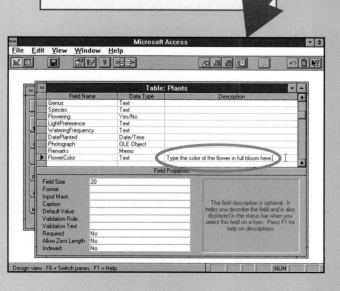

6 Type **Type the color of the flower in full bloom here.** as the descriptive text for the FlowerColor field.

NOTE ▼

Using descriptions for fields is optional. Access displays your description in the status bar whenever you place the cursor in the field. You can always change a field if you find that it doesn't meet your information needs.

TASK 9

Creating Number Type Fields

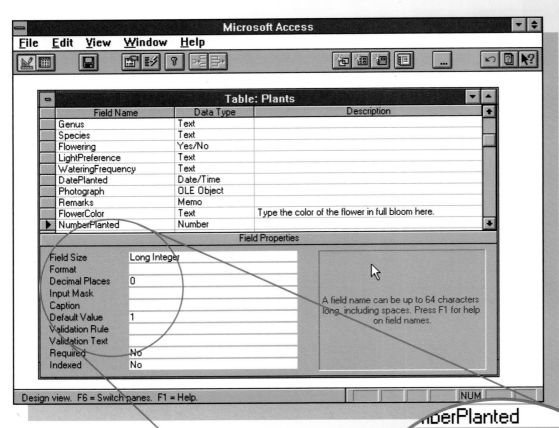

"Why would I do this?"

Number fields can contain only numeric information. Although this may seem limiting, number fields can be very useful. You can use a number field to calculate another number. You also can use this type of field for dates and currency.

In this task, you will create a number field.

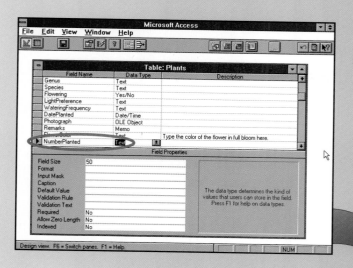

1 Click in the next blank field row. Type **NumberPlanted** and press the **Enter** key.

2 Click the **arrow** button in the Data Type field to display the drop-down menu, and click the **Number** option.

NOTE ▼

For a field that will contain only dates and/or time, select the Date/Time option. A date field can hold any date from January 1, 100 to December 31, 9999. If this field will be used only for dollar amounts, then select the Currency option. You can choose six currency formats and use a maximum of four decimal places.

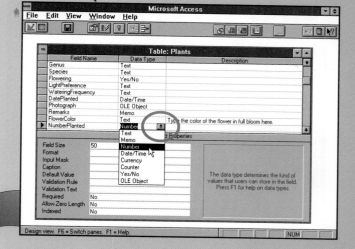

3 Press **F6**, or click the Field Size text box and click the **arrow** button to display the drop-down menu. Click the **Long Integer** option. This property enables you to select the type of number and the number range that can be entered into this field, not a certain number of characters. To find out what the choices mean, press the **F1** key to get Help about this topic.

Task 9: Creating Number Type Fields

4 Click the Decimal Places box. Click the **arrow** button and select the option **0**. Use this option to choose the number of decimal places that you want to allow in this field.

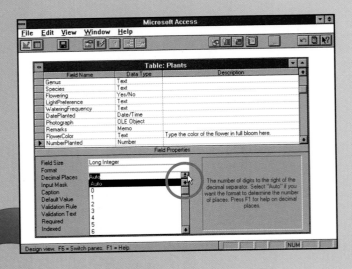

NOTE ▼

The Decimal Places property is dependent upon your selection made in Field Size. If you have chosen one of the three options that do not allow fractions in the Field Size property, then you will not be able to display a fraction.

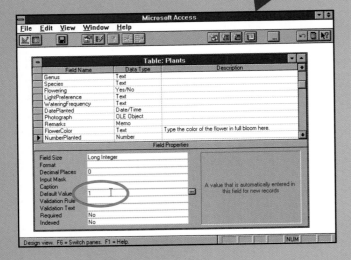

5 Click the mouse in the Default Value text box. Replace the 0 with the number 1, which causes Access for Windows to always enter the number 1 into this field. You can change this number if you have planted more than one plant.

WHY WORRY?

Remember, you can always go back and change a number if you find that the wrong number was entered, or if you let Access for Windows fill in a default value for you.

Using Yes/No Fields

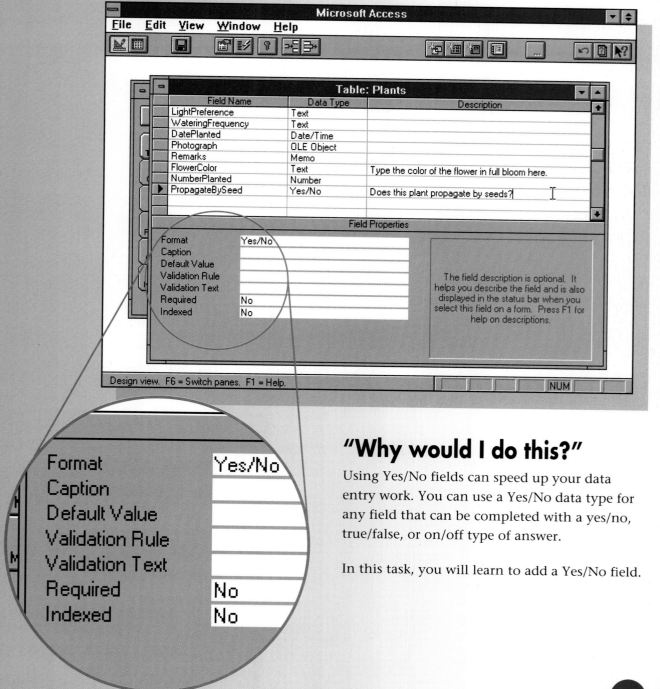

"Why would I do this?"

Using Yes/No fields can speed up your data entry work. You can use a Yes/No data type for any field that can be completed with a yes/no, true/false, or on/off type of answer.

In this task, you will learn to add a Yes/No field.

Task 10: Using Yes/No Fields

1 Move the cursor to the next blank field row. Type the field name **PropagateBySeed** and press **Enter**.

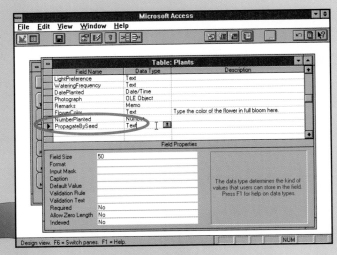

2 Click the **arrow** button in the Data Type field, then select the **Yes/No** option from the drop-down list.

NOTE ▼

If you know the name of the selection that you want to make from a drop-down list, you can select that item by typing the first letter or two. Access for Windows will fill in the rest for you. By typing the letter Y, Access for Windows fills in Yes/No.

3 Click the Field Properties Format option, and then click the **arrow** button. Select the **Yes/No** option, which is the most appropriate answer for this particular field.

WHY WORRY?

By using a Yes/No type of field, you can help eliminate data entry errors by allowing only one of two responses to a field.

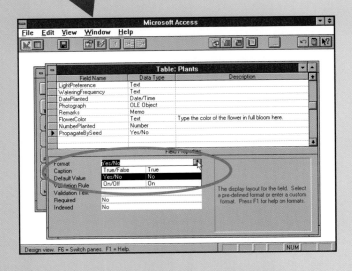

Saving Your New Table Definition

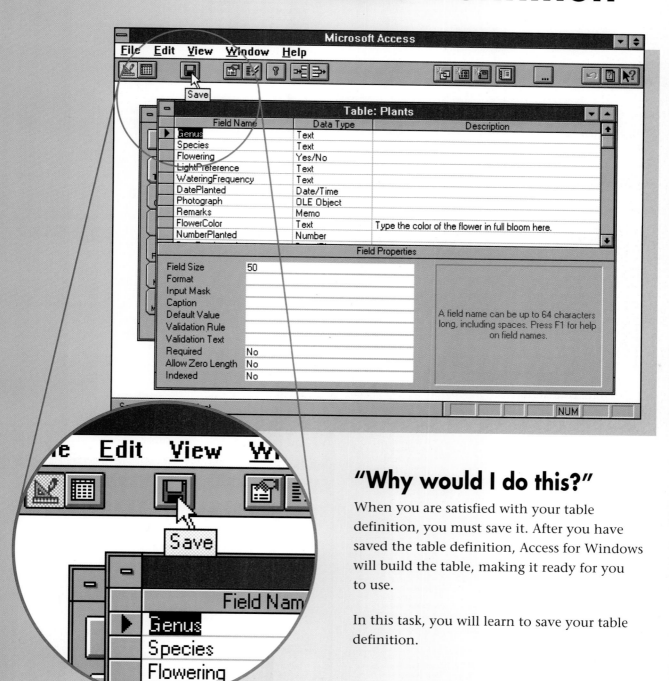

"Why would I do this?"

When you are satisfied with your table definition, you must save it. After you have saved the table definition, Access for Windows will build the table, making it ready for you to use.

In this task, you will learn to save your table definition.

Task 11: Saving Your New Table Definition

1 Click the **Save** button on the toolbar. If you watch closely, you will see different messages displayed in the status bar as Access for Windows completes each procedure necessary for saving your table definition.

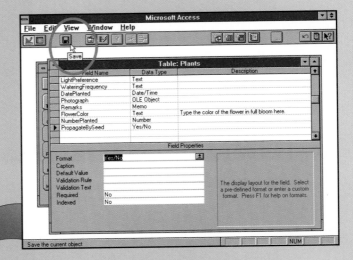

2 Click the **Control menu** button in the upper left corner of the Table window to display the Control menu. Click the **Close** option on the drop-down menu list to close the Plants Table window.

3 The Plants Table window is closed.

WHY WORRY?

If you were not yet finished with your table definition, you can stop at step 1 and continue to add or revise your table. Then save the table definition again.

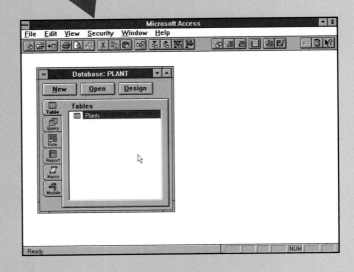

Opening a Database Table

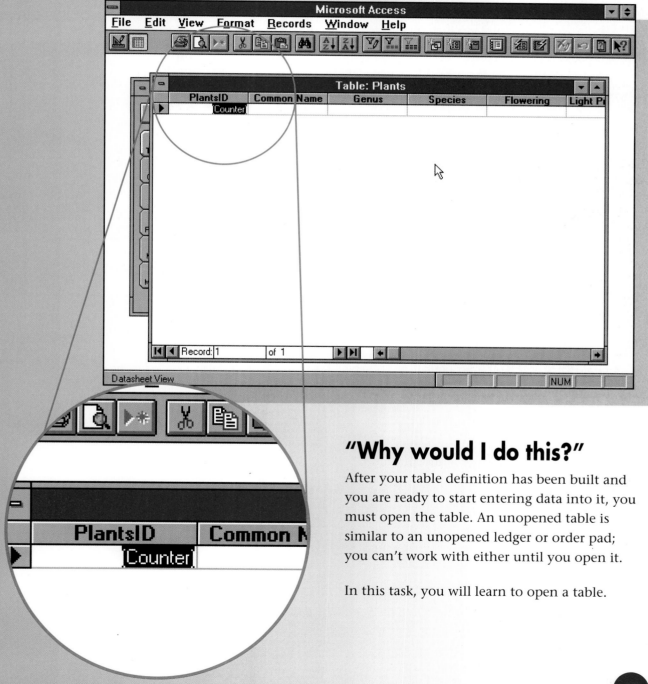

"Why would I do this?"

After your table definition has been built and you are ready to start entering data into it, you must open the table. An unopened table is similar to an unopened ledger or order pad; you can't work with either until you open it.

In this task, you will learn to open a table.

Task 12: Opening a Database Table

1 Click the **Table** button in the Database window. You will again see the list of available tables. Select the table from the list by clicking it or pressing the **up-arrow** key or the **down-arrow** key until the table to be selected is highlighted. Click the **Open** button in the Database window to open the Plants Table window in datasheet view.

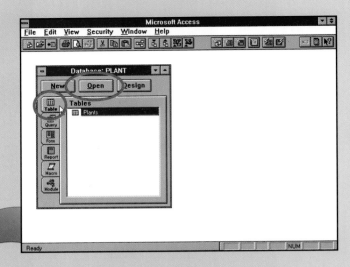

2 The Plants Table window is displayed in datasheet view.

> **NOTE** ▼
>
> Remember, you can also use the keyboard shortcut Alt+O to open the selected table.

Editing Field Names

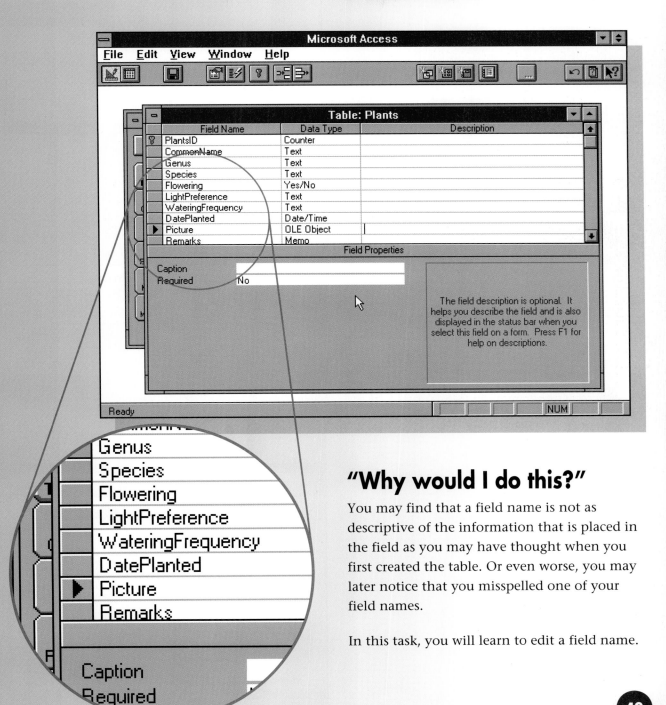

"Why would I do this?"

You may find that a field name is not as descriptive of the information that is placed in the field as you may have thought when you first created the table. Or even worse, you may later notice that you misspelled one of your field names.

In this task, you will learn to edit a field name.

Task 13: Editing Field Names

1 Click the **Table** button in the Database window, then highlight the table name that needs corrections. Click the **Design** button in the Database window.

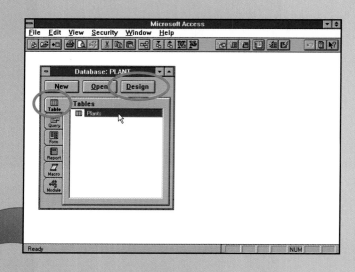

2 The selected table is opened in Design view.

> **NOTE** ▼
>
> Any time that you need to make a change to a table's definition, you must do so in Design view.

3 Select the field name to be edited by pressing the **up-arrow** key or **down-arrow** key, or by clicking the field name. Select the field name **Photograph**.

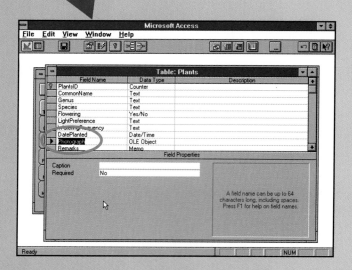

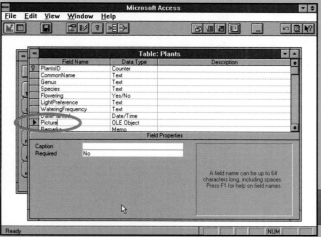

4 Type the new field name **Picture** over the old one. When the field name is highlighted, typing a new name completely replaces the previous name.

NOTE ▼

If you only have to change a single letter, or add to the end of the field name, position the I-bar mouse pointer at the position that you want to make your change and click. The horizontal cursor bar will be displayed at that location, enabling you to make any necessary changes.

5 Select the **Control menu** button in the Table window, then choose the **Close** option. You will be asked if you want to save changes. Choose **Yes** to save your changes.

WHY WORRY?

If you do not specifically save your changes, Access for Windows will tell you that you have made changes and ask if you do want to save them.

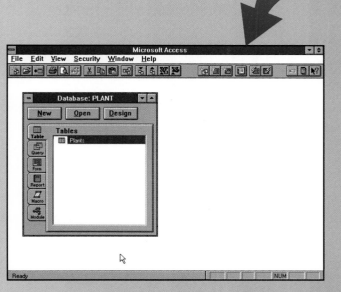

6 The table is saved and the window is closed.

Moving a Field in a Table

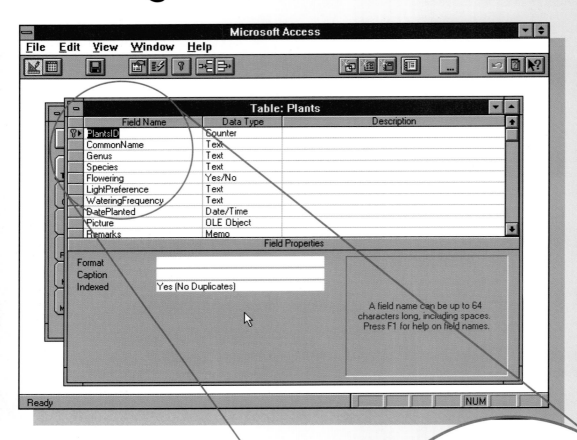

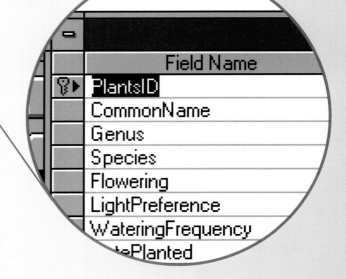

"Why would I do this?"

You may find that some of the fields aren't in the right place. For example, you may input data from a handwritten form that includes a client's social security number, last name, and first name. Your table's fields are sorted as first name, last name, and social security number. This discrepancy between the written form and your table requires some eyeball gymnastics that can get quite tiring by the end of a day.

In this task, you will learn to move a field from one location to another.

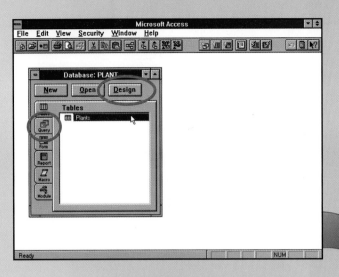

1 Click the **Table** button in the Database window, then select the table in which you want to move a field. Click the **Design** button in the Database window.

2 The selected table is opened in Design view.

> **NOTE** ▼
>
> To make a permanent change in the order of a field, open the table in Design view and reorder the fields to suit your needs.

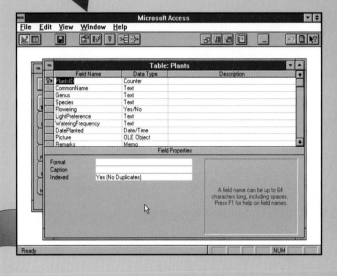

3 Click the **down-arrow** button on the scroll bar until the primary key field Flowering is displayed. You're going to move this field so that it is immediately after the CommonName field.

Task 14: Moving a Field in a Table

4 Move the mouse pointer to the record selector box to the left of Flowering, and click when the mouse pointer changes to a small black arrow. You will see that the entire row has been selected.

5 Place the mouse pointer on the selector box and drag it to its new position. You will see the arrow mouse pointer with a small gray box being dragged to the new position.

6 Release the mouse button to set the field in its new location underneath the CommonName field.

WHY WORRY?

If you drop the field in the wrong place, just move it again.

Inserting a Field

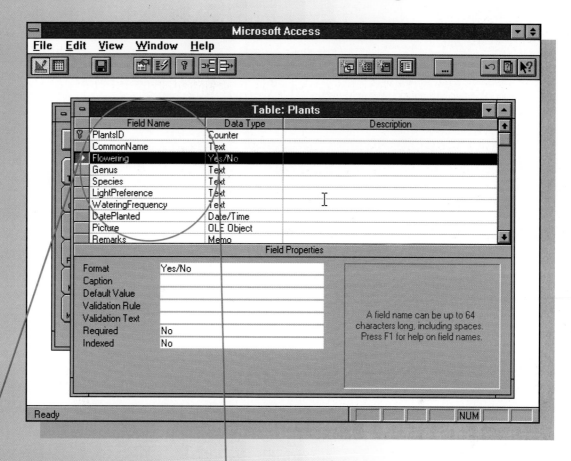

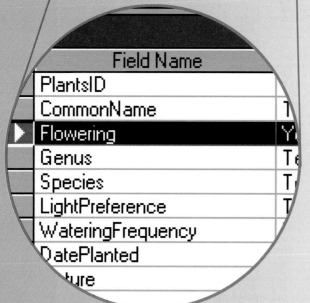

"Why would I do this?"

You may find that you want to add another field to your table. Instead of adding it to the end of your table and moving the field name to the location that you want, you can insert a blank line into your table definition and then enter the new table information—saving yourself several extra steps.

In this task, you will learn to insert a field into a table.

Task 15: Inserting a Field

1 Move the cursor until it is located on the field that will be below the newly inserted field.

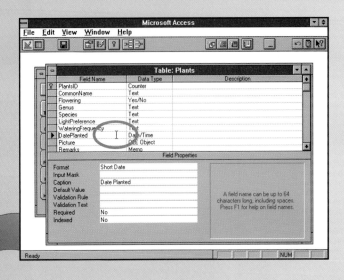

2 Move the mouse to the **Insert Row** button on the toolbar.

3 Click the **Insert Row** button. Access for Windows will insert a new blank row in the indicated position. You can now enter the required information for this field. Type **Location** and press the **Enter** key.

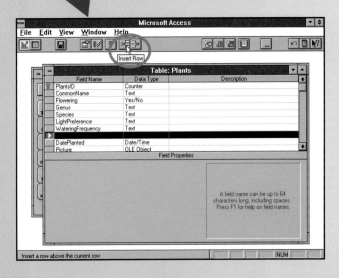

Deleting a Field

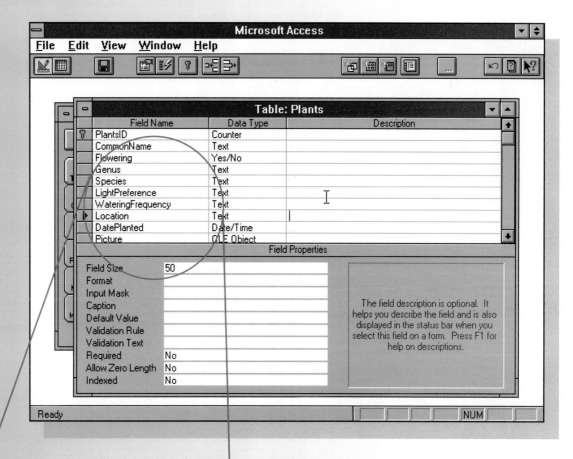

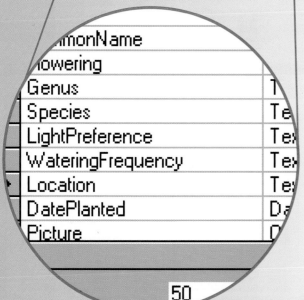

"Why would I do this?"

If you do not use the information in a field or you do not ever use the field, you can delete it from your table definition. You should be cautioned that just because you do not use the information in a given field, someone else who also uses the data contained in the table may use that particular field. Be sure that the information is not used before deleting it.

In this task, you will learn how to delete a row.

Task 16: Deleting a Field

1 Move the cursor until it is located on the Location field.

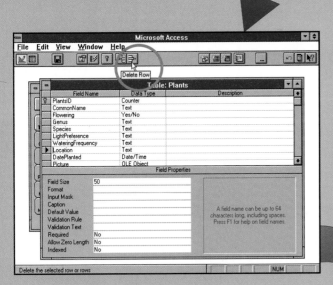

2 Move the mouse to the Delete Row button on the toolbar. Click the **Delete Row** button.

3 Access for Windows deletes the row and moves all rows that were below it up a position.

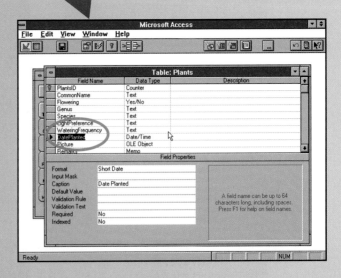

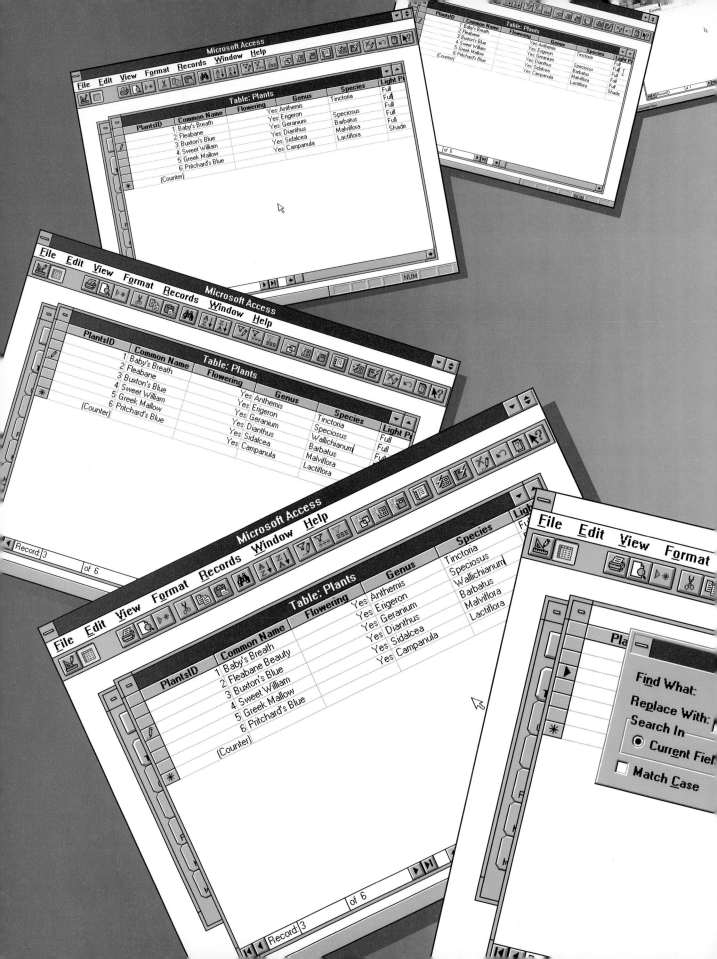

PART III

Entering and Editing Data

After you have created your database file and table, you can begin to enter information into it. When you add information to a table, you normally enter all the information for a single record, and then move to the next one. Remember, each row of the table is a single record. You can think of each record as a single, blank sheet of paper. When you have filled in the necessary information for the record, turn to the next blank page and enter the next record.

Each piece of the record is placed in its own field. Each field is contained on a single line of the paper. As you complete the information for a field, you move to the next line. In the Plants table that you created in Part II, you have fields for CommonName, for the Genus and Species, and other information related to each plant. Each page or record is numbered by the counter field called, PlantsID.

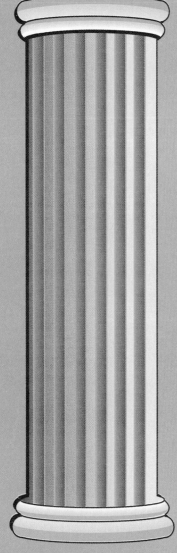

In a database file, you can easily add fields and records and change the information in them. You can change the appearance of your information by using a different font, change the height of your rows, or the width of a column. If necessary, you also can hide selected information from view. This can be especially helpful if you work with information of a more sensitive nature. If you work with personnel or payroll records and want to show a colleague some aspect of the information, but not specific personal data, you can hide the information from view.

The most common way that you will use to enter information in your Access for Windows table is by typing from the keyboard. After you have become more familiar with Windows and Access for Windows, you may want to enter information by importing information from other programs. You can even add pictures to your records.

The ability to quickly find and easily update your information as needed is one of the greatest features of using a database. With Access for Windows you can use the powerful Find command to search for a specific record or group of records.

Also, unlike your pad of records, each on their own individual page, you can easily sort all of your records in any way that you select. In the case of the Plants table, you can quickly sort the list of plants by common name, by genus, the date that you planted them, the number that you have planted, or by almost any other field that you want. You can sort your records in either an ascending or descending order. An ascending order is similar to a normal alphabetical order except that numbers come before letters. A descending order is the reverse of ascending, letters beginning with Z and ending with the number 0.

In Task 19 of this part, you will need to refer to the following tables. These tables include information that you will type to complete a database:

CommonName	Genus	Species	Flowering	Light Preference	Watering Frequency
Fleabane	Erigeron	Speciosus	Yes	Light Shade	Keep Moist
Buxton's Blue	Geranium	Wallichianum	Yes	Full	Dry Out Between
Sweet William	Diantus	Barbatus	Yes	Full	Keep Moist
Greek Mallow	Sidalcea	Malviflora	Yes	Full	Dry Out Between
Pritchard's Blue	Campanula	Lactiflora	Yes	Shade	Keep Moist

CommonName	Date	Picture	Remarks	FlowerColor	Number	Propagate BySeed
Fleabane	3/1/94		Herb Garden	Blue	56	yes
Buxton's Blue	3/10/94		Use as fill in	Blue	12	No
Sweet William	3/1/94			Pink	10	Yes
Greek Mallow	7/15/94			Yellow	12	Yes
Pritchard's Blue	2/15/94			Blue	8	Yes

TASK 17
Entering New Information

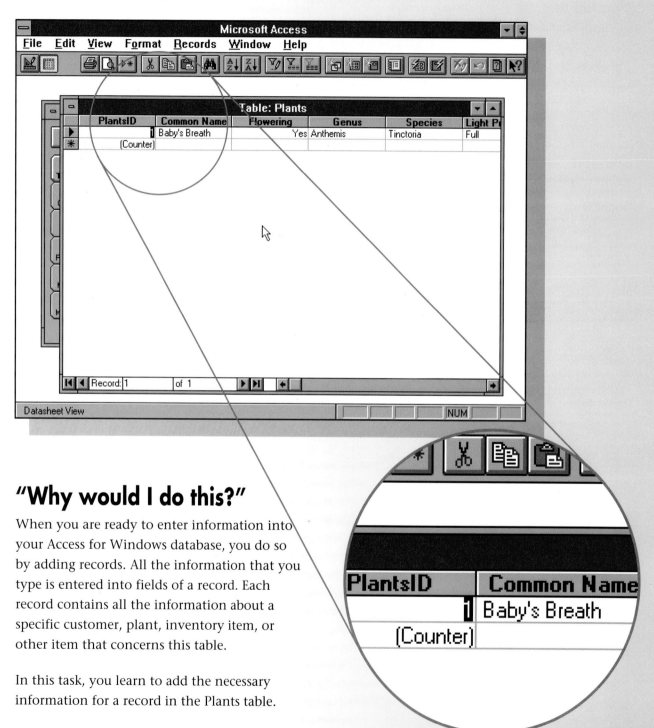

"Why would I do this?"

When you are ready to enter information into your Access for Windows database, you do so by adding records. All the information that you type is entered into fields of a record. Each record contains all the information about a specific customer, plant, inventory item, or other item that concerns this table.

In this task, you learn to add the necessary information for a record in the Plants table.

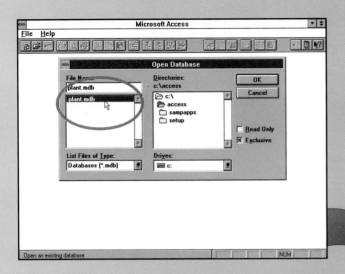

1 Click the **Open Database** button or press **Ctrl+O,** and then select the file PLANT.MBD from the file list box.

2 Click the **OK** button in the Open Database dialog box. This action opens the Database window. You always use this window to select the specific table that you want to work in.

3 Click the **Table** button to display the list of available tables, if necessary. Double-click the table Plants. This opens the Plants table. Because this table has not had any information entered into it previously, no records are displayed.

Task 17: Entering New Information

4 Press the **Enter** key once. This moves the cursor from the first field PlantsID to the next field CommonName. Type **Baby's Breath** and press the **Enter** key again. After you begin to type in the field CommonName, Access for Windows automatically enters the number in the first field PlantsID and creates a second blank record row.

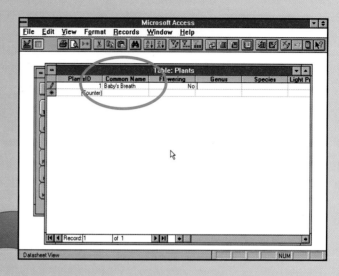

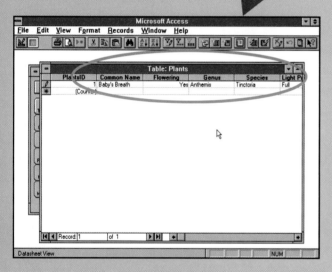

5 Enter the following information into the fields indicated: Flowering: **Yes**; Genus: **Anthemis**; Species: **Tinctoria**; LightPreference: **Full**; WateringFrequency: **Weekly**; DatePlanted: **3/1/94**; Remarks: **Border planting**; FlowerColor: **White**; NumberPlanted: **10**; PropagateBySeed: **Yes**. Be sure to press the **Enter** key as you finish the entry in each field. This moves the cursor to the next field.

NOTE ▼

You do not always have to enter information into every field (for example, the Picture field).

WHY WORRY?

If you mistype information in a field, simply highlight the information and retype it.

Copying Data from the Previous Record

"Why would I do this?"

At times, you will find that the information in a field, or several fields, is exactly the same record after record. Instead of retyping the information, you can copy the data between records. This saves you time and keeps you from mistyping the information.

In this task, you learn to copy information from one record to the next.

Task 18: Copying Data from the Previous Record

1 Click in the CommonName field of the blank record. Type **Fleabane** in the CommonName field, and **Eerigeron** in the Genus field, leave the Species field blank, and type **YES** in the Flowering field. Remember, you must press the **Enter** key to move between each field.

> **NOTE** ▼
> You can also use the Tab key to move from one field to the next. By using the key combination Shift+Tab, you can move to the previous field.

2 Move the mouse pointer to the LightPreference field in record number 1. Press and hold the left mouse button, and drag the I-bar shaped pointer across the word **Full**. The word is *highlighted* and shown as white text on a black background. When the word has been highlighted, it is *selected* and can be deleted or retyped.

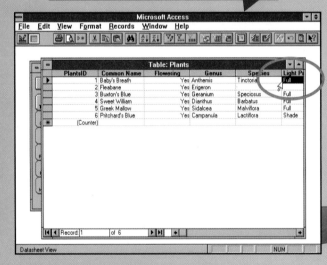

3 Select **Edit** from the main menu, and then **Copy** from the drop-down menu, or click the **Copy** button on the toolbar. These actions copy the selected text to the Windows Clipboard. This selected text remains on the Windows Clipboard until you replace it with other text.

4 Click in the empty field below the word Full.

5 Select **Edit** from the main menu, and then **Paste** from the drop-down menu, or click the **Paste** button on the toolbar. You immediately see the field filled in with the entry Full.

TASK 19

Moving Data to Another Record

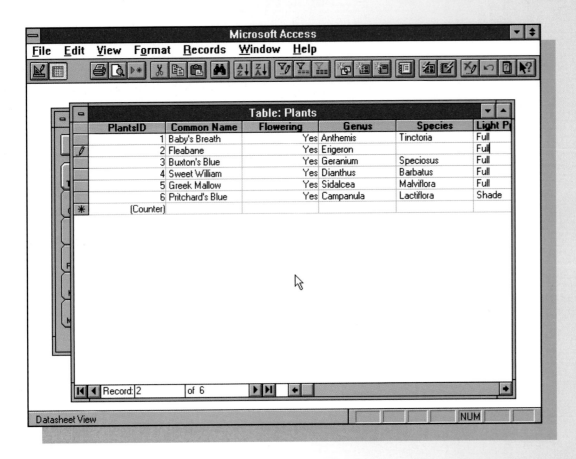

"Why would I do this?"

You may find that you have accidentally entered data into the wrong record. You can delete the information from the field, type the correct information, and then retype the information again in to the next record. You can also avoid some of these steps by simply moving the information to the next record, and then enter the correct information into the field.

In this task, you learn to move information from one record to another. Before you begin this task, enter the information included in the tables in the introduction to Part III.

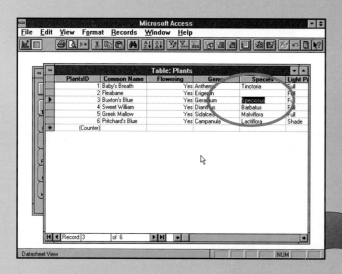

1 The information typed in the Species field for plant number 3 is actually for plant number 2. Move the cursor to the Species field for plant 3.

NOTE ▼

By pressing the up- and down-arrow keys to move between records, you automatically select the entry in the field as well. If you use the mouse to move the cursor to the field, you have to select the text also.

2 Select **Edit** from the main menu, and then **Cut** from the drop-down menu, or click the **Cut** button on the toolbar. You immediately see that Access for Windows deletes, or cuts the selected text from the table and places it on the Windows Clipboard.

WHY WORRY?

If you find that you cut the wrong information, simply move the cursor to the correct field and paste the information again.

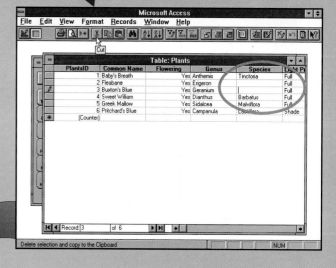

3 Press the **down-arrow** key once to move the cursor down to plant 13's row, and then click the **Paste** button on the tool-bar, or select **Edit** from the menu, and then **Paste** from the drop-down menu, or use the keyboard shortcut **Ctrl+V**. You see the cut text entered into the selected field.

Repeat these three steps to move the Species name from plant 12 to plant 13.

Editing Data in a Field

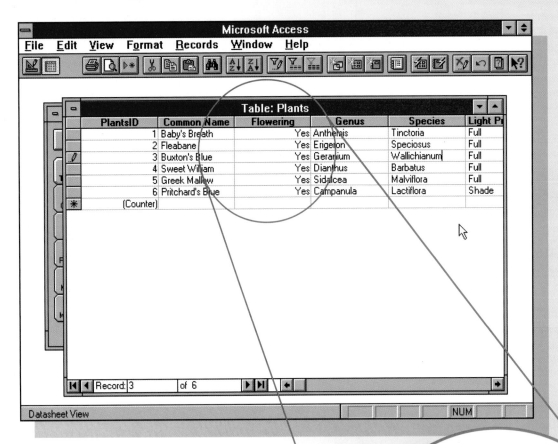

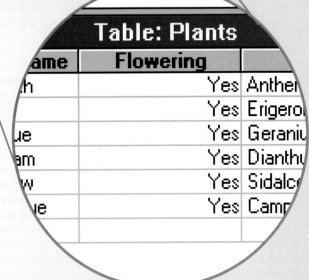

"Why would I do this?"

It is inevitable that you will find that your information has to be edited. You may find that an entry in a field was misspelled or a customer's address has changed, or you may have to add information to a record that you did not originally have.

For example, you have finally identified the specific type of "Fleabane" that you have in your garden. In this task, you add the Species name and add to the CommonName for this plant.

1 Move the mouse pointer to the right of the entry FLEABANE in the CommonName field, and click once. You see that a blinking, vertical edit cursor (insertion point) is displayed immediately after the last letter in FLEABANE.

2 Type **Beaauty**, and press the **Enter** key.

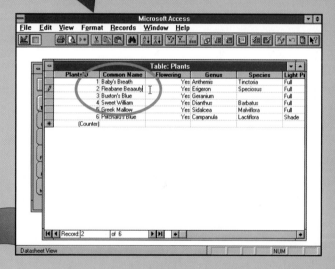

3 You see that you have misspelled the word Beaauty. Move the mouse pointer until it is directly between the two *a*'s.

Task 20: Editing Data in a Field

4 Click the left mouse button once. This places the blinking edit cursor between a's. Press the **Delete** key, this deletes the *a* to the right of the cursor.

NOTE ▼

You can also press the Backspace key and delete the A to the left of the cursor.

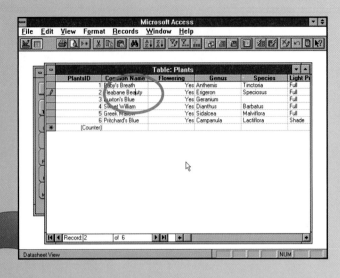

5 Move the cursor to the empty Species field. Type **Wallichianum**.

WHY WORRY?

There is no need to worry about your information becoming dated or errors remaining uncorrected when you can quickly and easily edit the information.

Undoing an Edit

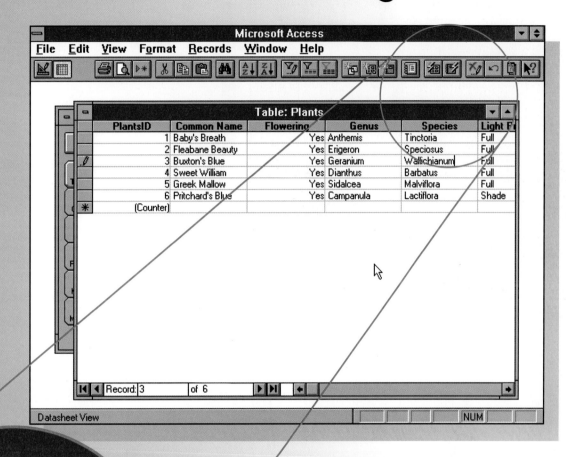

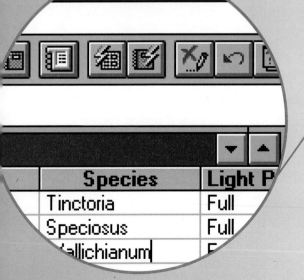

"Why would I do this?"

Any entry that you make in a field; entering new data, editing information, or adding additional information, can be undone—if you have not yet left the field. After you move the cursor to another field *within the same record*, you can undo all changes that you have made to the record since the last time that you saved the record. Access for Windows automatically saves a record if you leave the record or close the table.

In this task, you learn to undo changes to a field and a record.

Task 21: Undoing an Edit

1 To undo changes made in the field that you are currently in, click the **Undo** button on the toolbar. Now the last entry that you typed is deleted from the field.

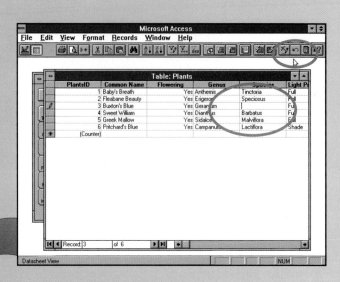

NOTE ▼

You can undo changes by selecting the Edit menu and then Undo Typing from the drop-down menu. This option changes names depending on the last action you have made. You can also use the keyboard shortcut Ctrl+Z to undo changes.

2 Restore the entry by clicking the **Undo** button again. You also can select **Edit** and then **Redo Typing** from the menu, or press **Ctrl+Z**.

3 Delete all changes made to a record by clicking the **Undo Current Field/ Record** button on the toolbar, or press **Esc**.

WHY WORRY?

Usually you can use the Undo Current Field/Record button to restore the items that you have deleted using the Undo feature.

Searching for and Replacing Selected Data

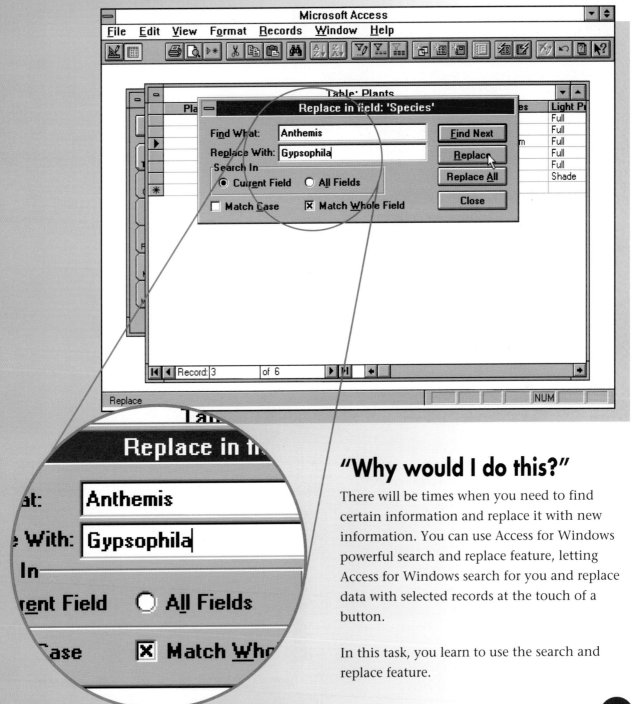

"Why would I do this?"

There will be times when you need to find certain information and replace it with new information. You can use Access for Windows powerful search and replace feature, letting Access for Windows search for you and replace data with selected records at the touch of a button.

In this task, you learn to use the search and replace feature.

Task 22: Searching for and Replacing Selected Data

1 Click in the Genus field of the first record, and select **Edit** from the main menu, then select **Replace** from the drop-down menu, or press the shortcut combination **Ctrl+H**. The Replace dialog box is displayed.

NOTE ▼

The fastest way to conduct a search and replace is to work in a single field. Access for Windows allows you to search all fields if you are not sure which field the information is in.

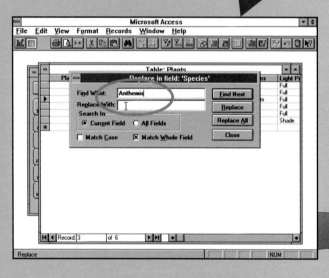

2 You realize that the wrong Genus name has been entered for a plant, and you want to search for and then replace the incorrect name with the correct information. Type **Anthemis** in the Find What text box, and press the Tab key to move to the next text box.

3 Type **Gypsophila** in the **Replace With** text box.

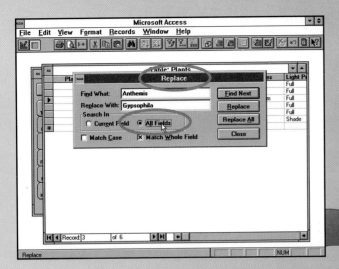

4 If you want to search in all fields of your table, click the **All Fields** radio button. Notice that the name of the dialog box in the title bar changes when you select this radio button option.

5 You can click the **Match Case** option box to tell Access for Windows to find only those instances that exactly match what you have typed in the Find What text box. When turned off, or unchecked, the entry you have made, Anthemis, finds Anthemis, anthemis, and ANTHEMIS. If you turn on the **Match Case** option, you find only those entries that have identical upper- and lowercase.

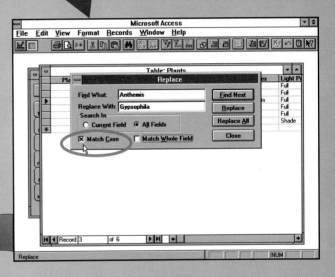

6 You can click the **Match Whole Field** option box to tell Access for Windows to find only those fields that match the entry in the Find What text box, word for word. You do not necessarily have to match upper- and lowercase letters, but all the words must be there.

7 Click the **Find Next** button in the Replace dialog box. It is not obvious whether Access for Windows found a match or not, except you notice that the current record indicator, the arrowhead in the left column, has moved down.

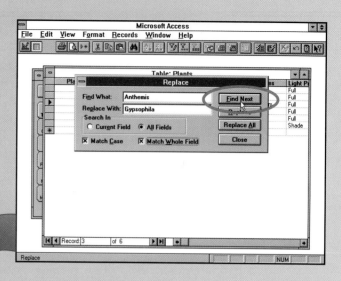

NOTE ▼

Always be sure to start your searches at the beginning of your records. Do this by placing the cursor in the first row of the field to be searched.

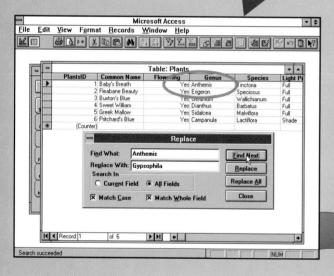

8 Move the mouse pointer to the title bar of the dialog box, and drag it down until it is below the record line with the arrow, and then release the mouse button. This, unfortunately, is not the record that you want to replace with the new information.

9 Click the **Find Next** button again to search for the next occurrence of the item you entered in the Find What text box. Access for Windows has searched to the end of the records in this table. Since you may have started the search with a record that was not the very first record in the table, you will want to start at the beginning and try again.

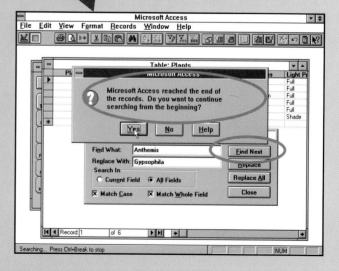

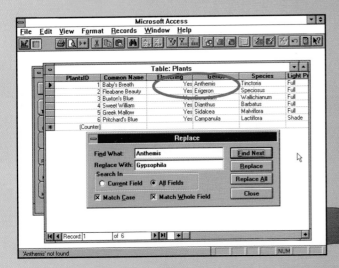

10 Click the **Yes** button in the dialog box. You will now see that Access for Windows has found another occurrence of the text that you entered in the Find What text box.

11 Click the **Replace** button in the Replace dialog box. You can see that Access for Windows has replaced the incorrect, or old text, with the replacement text. You also notice that Access for Windows immediately goes to find the next occurrence of the Find What text and highlights it again. Click the **Close** button to stop the search and replace function and return to the table.

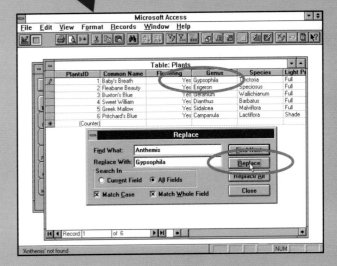

Sorting Records

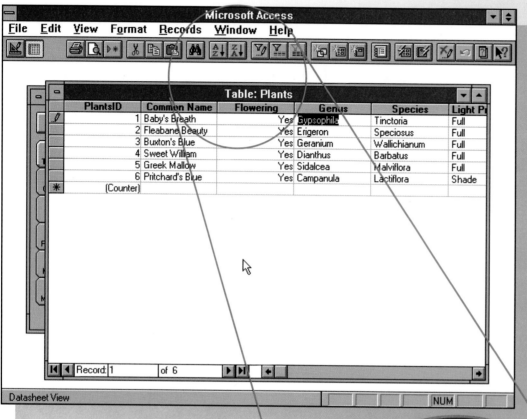

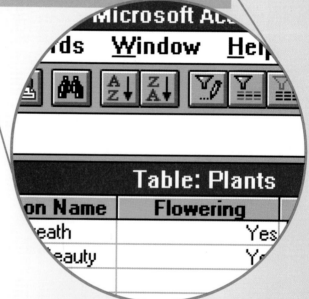

"Why would I do this?"

Access for Windows normally sorts the information in your table by the leftmost column—the first field of each record. In most cases, you have allowed Access for Windows to automatically assign a number for each record. If you want to view the plants listed in your table, you probably want to see them in alphabetical order—not number order. To see them in alphabetical order, you sort the table using either the CommonName field or the Genus field. In this task, you sort the table by the Genus field.

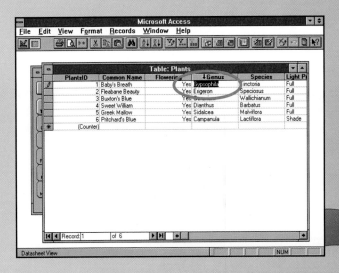

1 Move the mouse pointer to the field name Genus. The mouse pointer changes to a small, downward facing arrow.

2 Click the left mouse button. This selects the column. The column is now highlighted.

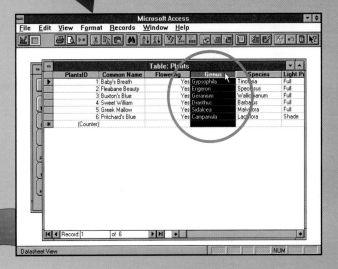

3 Click the **Sort Ascending** button on the toolbar. Access for Windows immediately re-sorts your table in alphabetical order using the selected field Genus.

> **NOTE** ▼
>
> You can also sort a column in descending order by clicking the Sort Down button on the toolbar.

Deleting a Record

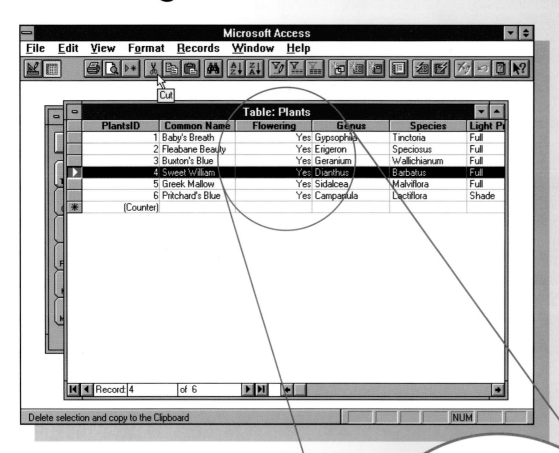

"Why would I do this?"

As you add records to your table, there will come a time when some of your records are no longer used. This may be due to information that is out-of-date for many reasons. For example, a customer no longer buys from you, you no longer buy a certain inventory item, or in the case of your plants list, you no longer grow a certain plant. When this occurs, you may want to delete these records.

In this task, you learn to delete selected records.

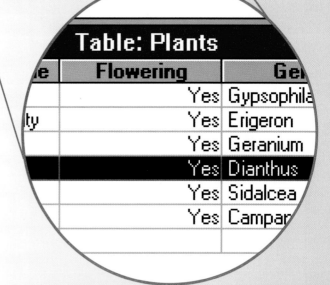

1 Move the mouse pointer to the record selector box for plant number 4. Notice how the mouse pointer changes shape to a right-facing arrow.

2 Click the left mouse button once. You see the entire record has been selected.

NOTE ▼

You can easily deselect a record by clicking the mouse pointer on any field. This removes the highlight from the record.

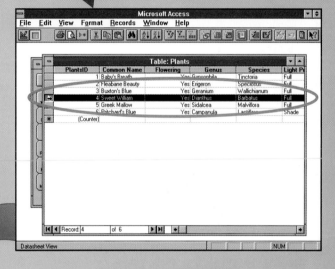

3 Press the **Delete** key on your keyboard. Access for Windows deletes the selected record from your table, and you now see a dialog box that tells you that you have just deleted a record. If you are sure that you want to delete this record, then click the **OK** button. Otherwise, click the **Cancel** button, and Access for Windows restores the record. You also can delete a selected record by clicking the **Cut** button on the toolbar.

Moving Field Columns

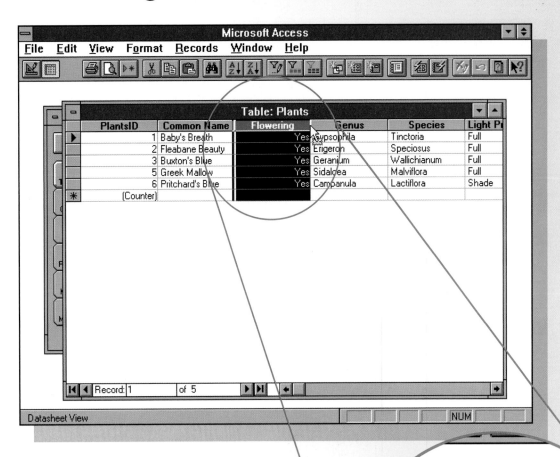

"Why would I do this?"

After you have worked with your table for a time, you may find that the order of your fields is not the way that you naturally view or enter information. If, for example, all of your catalogs and reference books always refer to the genus and species of a plant and then give various common names later in the text, ordering your table first by common name and then genus and species is not the best arrangement.

In this task, you learn to move a column and save the new order.

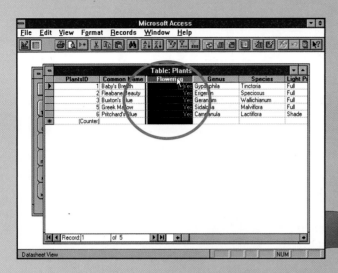

1 Move the mouse pointer to the field name Flowering, and click the left mouse button. This selects the entire column.

2 Click and hold the left mouse button, and drag the column to its new location. Notice that the mouse pointer adds a small box below the arrow. This represents the column that is being moved. As you drag the mouse pointer over a column margin, it becomes a solid thick bar. This represents a drop point. You can drop and insert the column at any of these points. If you want to save this new arrangement permanently, select the File Save Table command or press **Ctrl+S**.

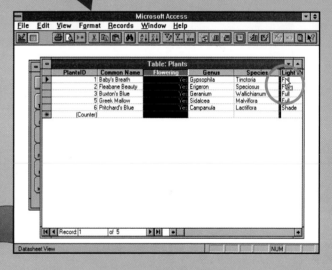

3 Drop the column between the fields Species and LightPreference by letting go of the left mouse button. You now see the column moved to its new location.

WHY WORRY?

If this is not the correct location for this column, drag and drop it to the correct place.

Resizing Rows or Columns

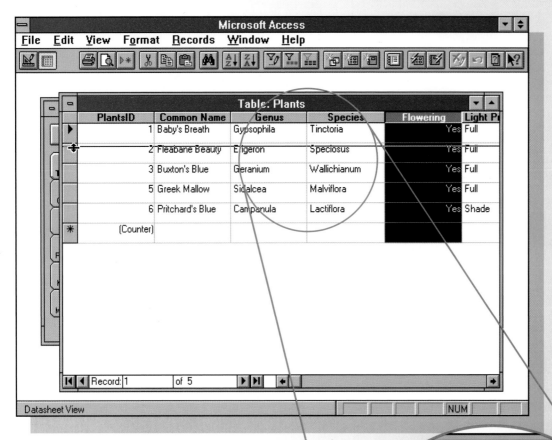

"Why would I do this?"

Access for Windows makes all columns the same width to begin with. If information does not fit within a column, or a column is too wide for the information, you can expand or contract the column. Alternatively, if the font used to display your text is too small, or you would prefer more space separating your rows, you can increase your row height.

In this task, you learn to change a row's height and a column's width.

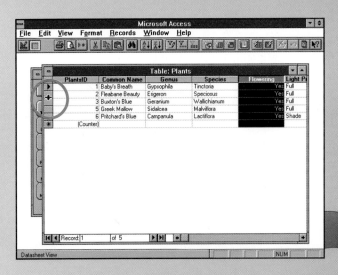

1 To change the row height of your record lines, move the mouse pointer to any record selection box, and move the cursor up or down until it changes shape to a line with up and down facing arrows.

2 Press the left mouse button and drag the mouse pointer down. This increases the row height. Notice the dark line extending from the drag pointer. This indicates the current width of your row.

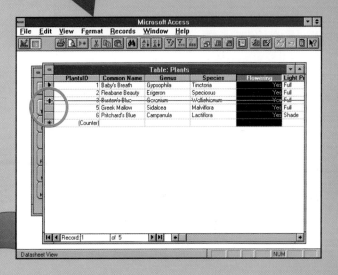

3 Release the mouse button. You now see the row height changed to the size you have indicated. By increasing the row height, you can add additional white space to the records, giving yourself a less-cramped appearing table. Changes made to row height affect all the rows in your table. You can decrease the space between rows by simply dragging any row divider line up.

Task 26: Resizing Rows or Columns

4 Move the mouse pointer to the dividing line between field names. The pointer changes shape again to a solid vertical line with two arrows pointing to the left and right.

NOTE ▼

Always select the dividing line to the right of the column whose size you want to adjust.

5 Press the left mouse button and drag the pointer to the left to make the column narrower, and drag it to the right to make the column wider. Notice the solid line extending from the resize pointer, indicating the new column width.

WHY WORRY?

You can expand and contract columns and row width at any time. The size of the column or row does not affect the information that is contained in the field or record.

6 Release the mouse button to set the new column size. Notice how Access for Windows has automatically adjusted the text in this column to fit the available space, by making two lines.

NOTE ▼

If you still had the row adjusted to the narrower width, the text appears to be cut off at the column border line. The text is not deleted, only hidden. To see all the text, expand the column width.

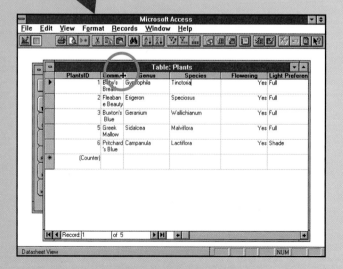

Freezing and Unfreezing Columns

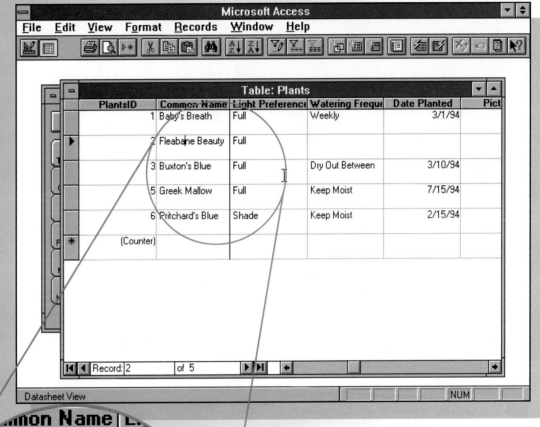

"Why would I do this?"

If you are entering information in a table that is very wide, the information in the first several columns quickly scrolls off the screen so that you can no longer see them. You can freeze any column as the leftmost column. This column then is always visible, allowing you to have a reference field at all times.

In this task, you learn to freeze and then unfreeze selected columns.

Task 27: Freezing and Unfreezing Columns

1 Move the mouse pointer to the column selector or field name for the field PlantsID, and click. This action selects the column.

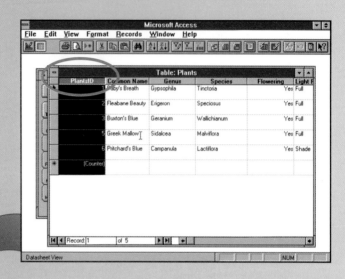

2 Move the pointer to the next column selector, CommonName. Press and hold the **Shift** key as you click the left mouse button and drag across to select both columns to select all columns. These columns give you enough information to know which plant you are working with when you have scrolled across the table.

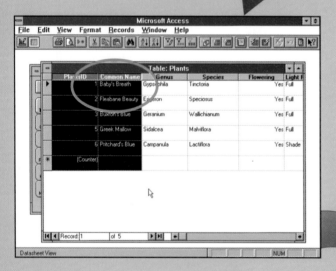

3 Select **Format** from the main menu and then **Freeze Columns** from the drop-down menu. Click the mouse anywhere in the table to remove the highlight from the columns. You now see a solid border line between the columns that are frozen and those that are not.

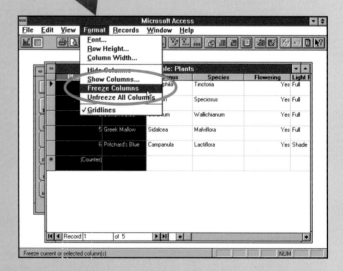

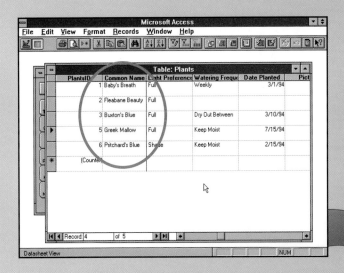

4 Press the **Enter** or **Tab** key to scroll through the fields of your table. Notice how the first three fields that have been frozen remain in place, whereas the others move across your screen.

5 Select **Format** from the menu and then **Unfreeze All Columns** from the drop-down menu. Access for Windows removes the solid dividing line and restores the table to normal scrolling.

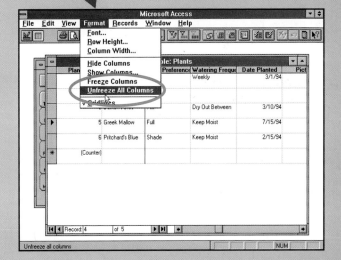

NOTE ▼

You can also select a middle column to freeze as your reference column, for example the column CommonName. Access for Windows automatically moves this column to the leftmost position in the table. After you unfreeze the columns, you have to drag the column back to its normal position.

Hiding and Unhiding Columns

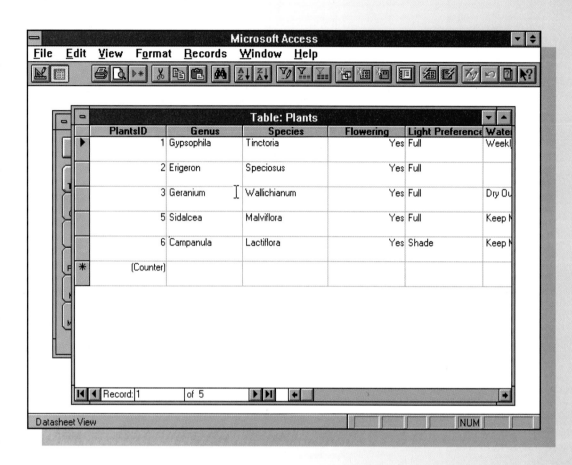

"Why would I do this?"

If you are working with sensitive information, you may want to hide columns from view if you are showing a coworker part of your table. For example, if you are showing a customer your inventory table, you may want to hide the column that contains your cost information.

In this task, you learn to hide and then expose a column from view.

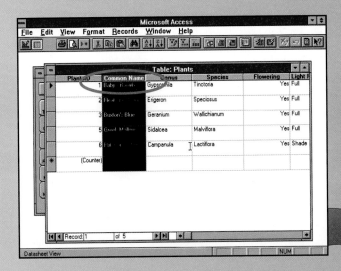

1 Select the column to be hidden by clicking the column selector. This highlights the entire column.

NOTE ▼

You can select more than one adjacent column at a time, by clicking and then dragging across the column selectors.

2 Select **Format** from the main menu and then **Hide Columns** from the drop-down menu. You now see that the selected column, CommonName, has been hidden from view.

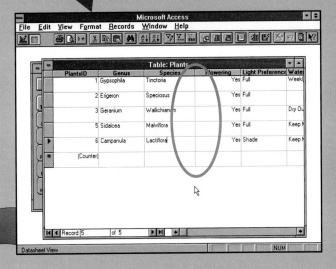

3 Select **Format** from the main menu and then **Show Columns** from the drop-down menu. The Show Columns dialog box is now displayed. Notice that this dialog box has a button for both Hide and Show. Also notice that in the Column list box all the column names are checked except the hidden field, CommonName.

4 To show or unhide a hidden column, select it from the Column list box and click the **Show** button. If you do not see the name of the column in the list, use the scroll bar to view the other column names. The name is selected when the highlighted box is on it. You now can see that the CommonNamecolumn is now displayed behind the Show Columns dialog box.

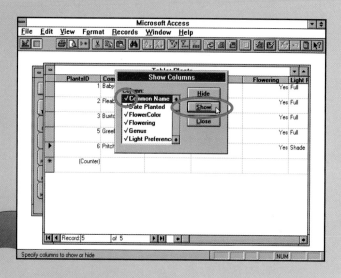

> **NOTE** ▼
>
> Any column that does not have a check mark displayed beside it is a hidden column.

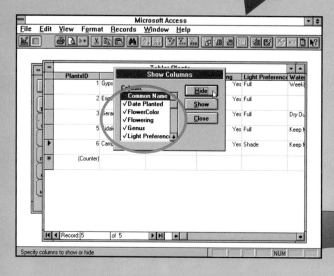

5 You can select multiple column names from the list by dragging the mouse pointer across them. Here you see the next five names on the list selected.

6 Click the **Hide** button. Notice how several columns that were displayed behind the dialog box have now been hidden. Also notice that the column names displayed in the list box no longer have check marks beside them. Click the **Show** button to redisplay the hidden columns. Click the **Close** button to remove the Show Columns dialog box from the screen.

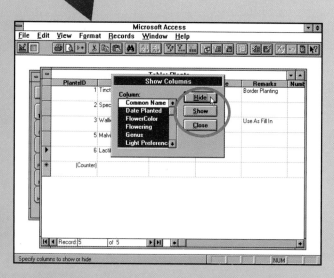

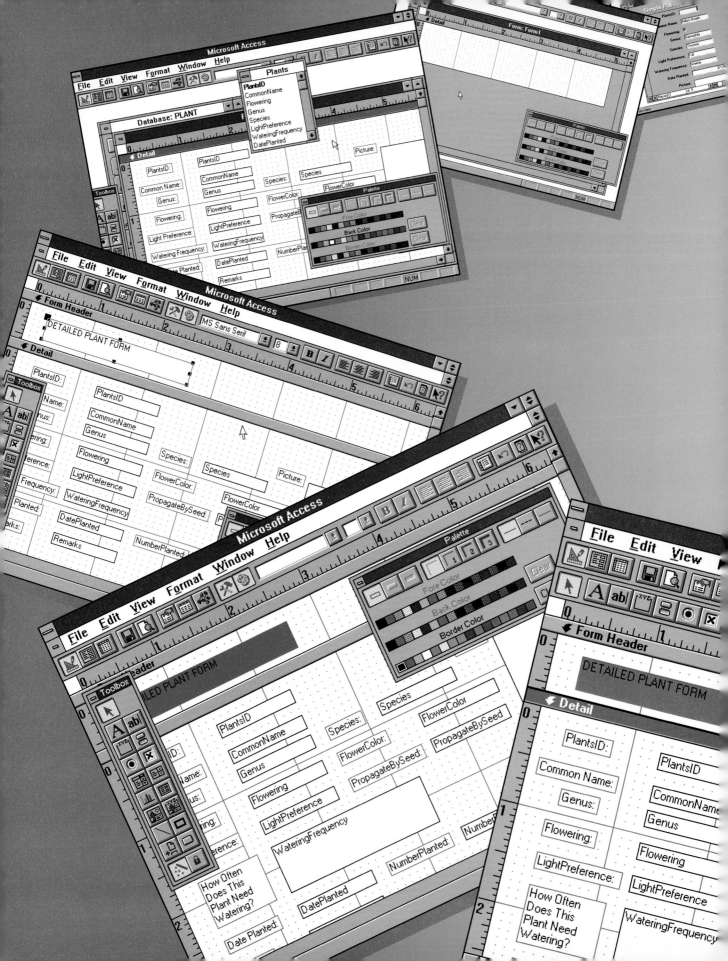

PART IV

Using Database Forms

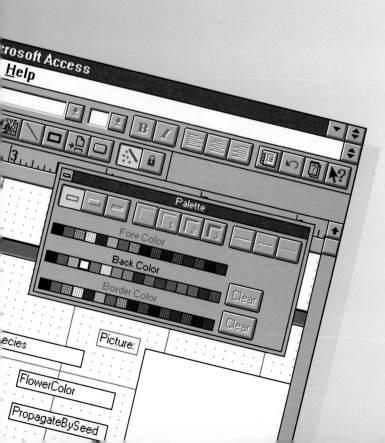

You have now learned to use an Access for Windows table to view, enter, and edit your information. With Access for Windows, you have another method of manipulating the information in your table—by using a form.

Most of us find the form is more user-friendly because it is a more familiar format for displaying and using information. The form can be a simple on-screen representation of a form that you use daily at work. Each record is presented on its own form or page. If you need to see more than a single record at a time, you can easily switch to the Datasheet mode with the click of a button.

A form is often more convenient to use because you can view all the fields for a single record at one time. You won't have to scroll around on the table to view the different fields of a record. When you design or customize a form, you can move fields to locations that you are more accustomed to. You can also create fields that require you to make a single selection from several options. By using labels you can easily distinguish what type of information is needed in a field.

You can draw on your form, helping to separate sections from each other. You also can use color, 3-D effects, and different fonts to distinguish different parts of your form from each other. Creating a visually attractive and well-designed form is not only a sign of your professionalism, but it usually makes the form easier to work with.

Forms are created in one of two different ways; you can use the Form Wizards to help you to design a form, or you can use the Form Designer window and create your form from scratch. For your first few forms, you might find it is easier to begin by using the Form Wizard rather than a blank design forms window.

The Form Wizard is the simplest way to create a form. The Form Wizard asks you questions about the type of form you want to create, what table you want to base the form on, and the type of form layout that you want to use. You then can select the fields to be included on your form—you do not have to include all fields from a table in a form. You also can choose a style for your fields and labels that includes:

Style	How It Will Look on Your Form
Standard	Your information is displayed directly to the right of the field name. There are no other enhancements to the field name or information.
Chiseled	A line is placed beneath your information, giving the form an appearance of a three-dimensional chiseled line. Field names and your information seem to be printed on the form.
Shadowed	Your information is displayed in a box with a shadow behind the box, giving the appearance that your information is floating above the form. Field names appear printed on the form.
Boxed	A box is displayed surrounding both your field name and your information. Field names and information are displayed in different colors and fonts.
Embossed	Your information is displayed in a box with an embossed or indented three-dimensional effect. Your field names are not embellished.

You can even add enhancements to a form—like a form title or, if necessary, a short block of instructions to other users of your form.

Creating a Form with the Form Wizard

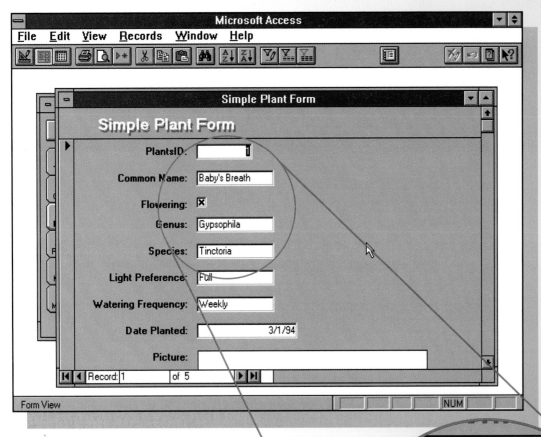

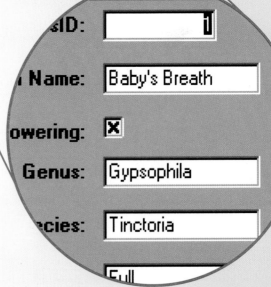

"Why would I do this?"

Using the Form Wizard is the easiest way to create a simple form. You can choose from several layouts for your form and select the specific fields to be included on the form from your table.

In this task, you learn to open and use the Form Wizard to create a form.

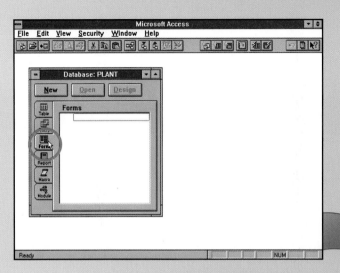

1 From the Database window, click the **Form** button. The Forms list is displayed in the Database window. Since you have not yet created a form, this list is empty.

2 Click the **New** button. The New Form dialog box is displayed.

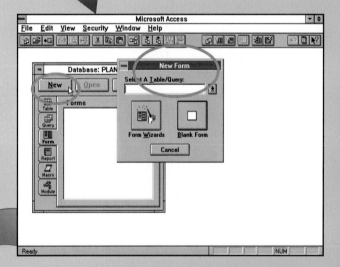

3 Click the Select A Table/Query **down-arrow** button to display the list of Tables or Queries that you can use to base your form on. Because you only have created a single table, you only see the single choice of Plants. Click this table name. Access for Windows adds it to the text box. Click the **Form Wizards** button.

4 You now see another dialog box. You have five options for the type of form you can create. The easiest and most common is the Single-Column form. This form displays selected fields of your table in a single column with the field name displayed on the left of the field. The AutoForm option creates a form similar to the Single-Column option with all fields included. Select the Single-Column option by double-clicking it.

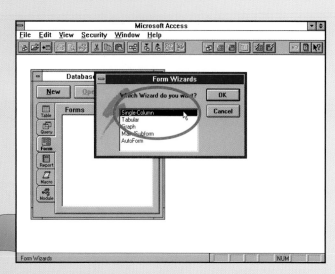

5 You now see the Microsoft Access Form Wizard dialog box. From this dialog box select the fields from the table to be included in the form. Include an individual field by clicking it with the mouse from the Available fields list box. Then click the > button to add the field to the Field order on form list box.

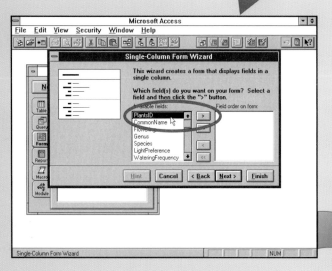

6 As you add a field to the Field order on form list box, it is removed from the Available fields list box.

> **NOTE** ▼
>
> The fields that you add are in the sequence that they will be displayed on your form. You choose the order for your fields by placing them in the order that you want them displayed.

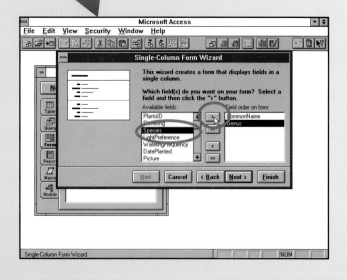

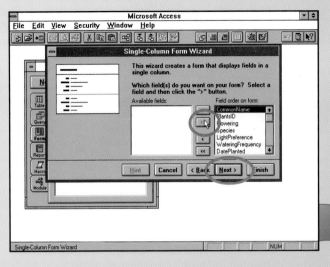

7 Click the >> button to include the remaining fields on your form. Click the **Next >** button to move to the next step. The Microsoft Access Form Wizard dialog box is displayed.

NOTE ▼

Use the < button to remove a selected field from the Field order on form list. The << button removes all the fields from the Field order on form list and places them back in the Available fields list. Use this option if you want to start over.

8 You use this dialog box to select the style of form that you want to use. You have five styles to choose from: Standard, Chiseled, Shadowed, Boxed, and Embossed. For this example, use the default selection Embossed. Click the **Next >** button in this dialog box.

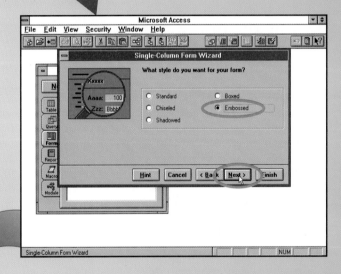

9 You now see the final Microsoft Access Form Wizard dialog box. **Type Simple Plant Form** in the text box at the top of the dialog box. This is the title for your form. Click the **Finish** button to display your new form.

10 You now see your form on-screen with the first record from your table displayed in it.

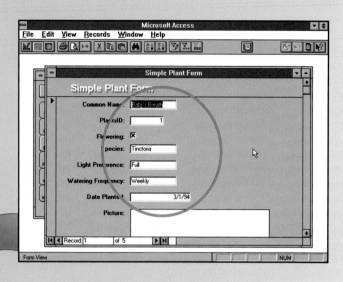

11 Click the mouse pointer on the Simple Plant Form window's Control menu button. Remember, this is the small button in the upper left corner of the window. Select the **Close** option from the drop-down menu. Click the **Yes** button to save your new form.

NOTE ▼

Always use a name for your form that helps you to remember its purpose. This way you won't have to open several forms to find the one you want to use.

12 You then see the Save As dialog box. Type **Simple Plant Form** in the text box. This is now the name for this form. Click the **OK** button to save the form and the new form name.

WHY WORRY?

As you work your way through the Form Wizard dialog boxes, you can use the < Back button to go back to the previous dialog box, if you need to change an option that you have already selected.

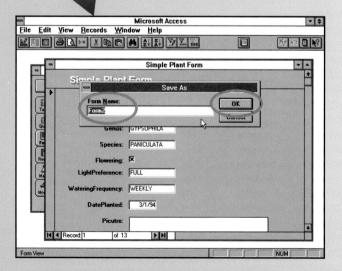

Opening a Blank Form

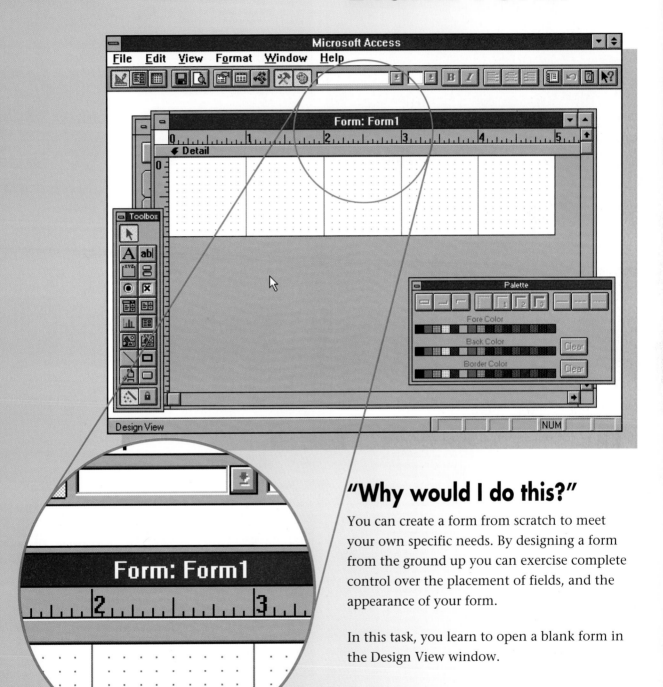

"Why would I do this?"

You can create a form from scratch to meet your own specific needs. By designing a form from the ground up you can exercise complete control over the placement of fields, and the appearance of your form.

In this task, you learn to open a blank form in the Design View window.

Task 30: Opening a Blank Form

1 From the Database window, click the **Form** button. You see the Forms list displayed in the Database window. This list now displays the form name that you just created.

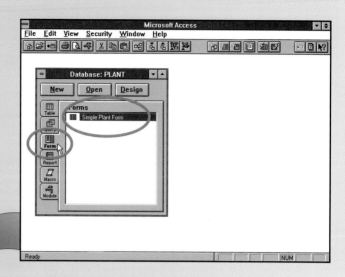

2 Click the **New** button. This again opens the New Form dialog box. Select the Plants table from the Select A Table/Query list by clicking the **down-arrow** button beside the text box. This is the table that you want to use to base your form on. Click the **Blank Form** button.

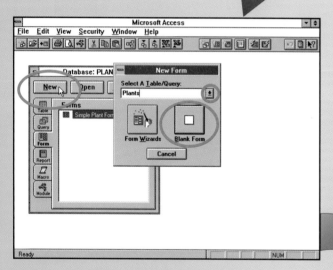

3 You now see a blank form in the Design View window. From this window you can create your own form.

WHY WORRY?

Access displays a toolbox and a palette when you are in Design view. Display the toolbox or palette by choosing it from the View menu. If either one is on top of something, move it around the screen by dragging the title bar to a new place. To close either one, click the Control menu box.

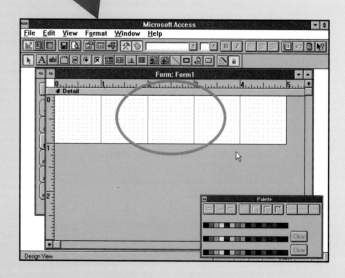

Adding Table Fields to a Form

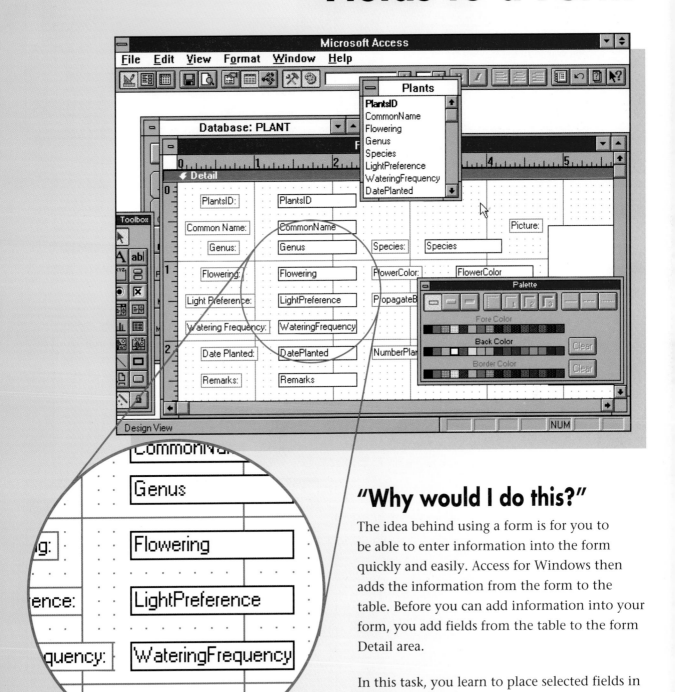

"Why would I do this?"

The idea behind using a form is for you to be able to enter information into the form quickly and easily. Access for Windows then adds the information from the form to the table. Before you can add information into your form, you add fields from the table to the form Detail area.

In this task, you learn to place selected fields in the Detail area of your form.

Task 31: Adding Table Fields to a Form

1 Click the **Field List** button on the first toolbar. You see the pop-up dialog box listing the available fields that you can use for your form.

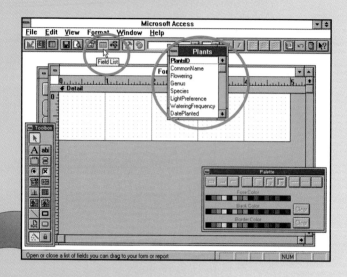

> **NOTE** ▼
>
> You can easily remove the Field List dialog box from the screen by clicking the Field List button again.

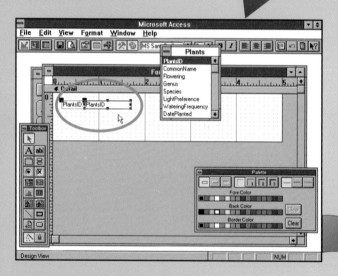

2 Select a field that you want to include on your form. For example, click and drag the field PlantsID from the list box to the white-dotted Detail area of the Design View window.

> **NOTE** ▼
>
> When you place a field, you see that there are two boxes with the same name in them. The box on the left is the label box, while the one on the right is the actual field box. When you complete your form, the label box still contains the label for the field, while the field box is blank.

3 Release the mouse button once you have the field placed in the location that you want. You can move a field by clicking it and then dragging it to another location. Notice how the mouse pointer has changed shape to a small open-palmed hand. When the pointer changes to this shape you can move both the label and field boxes to a new location.

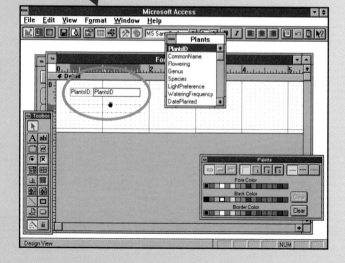

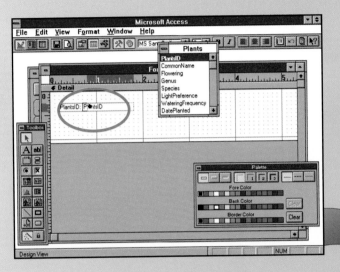

4 To move just one or the other box, point to the large move handle box, located in the upper left corner of both the label and field boxes. The pointer again changes shape to a small hand with an extended index finger. You can now drag either one of the boxes without the other.

5 Enlarge the Detail area by dragging the edges of the Detail area with the mouse pointer. You can increase the length of your form by dragging the bottom edge. Expand the width of your form by dragging the right edge. Increase both edges at the same time by dragging the bottom right corner.

NOTE ▼

You can also enlarge a field by clicking it and then dragging any of the black resizing handles that surround the field.

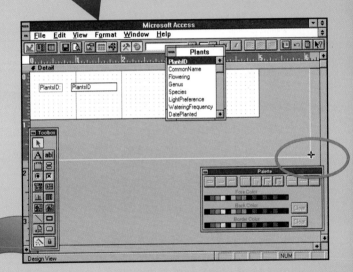

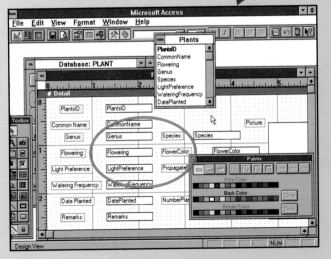

6 Drag the remaining fields onto your form. Notice how your fields are neatly aligned with the rows of dots or gridlines on the Detail area. The rows of dots and lines act like magnets and attract your fields to the closest part of the grid. This is called *Snap to Grid*; it helps you adjust and align your fields.

111

TASK 32

Creating a Label Box

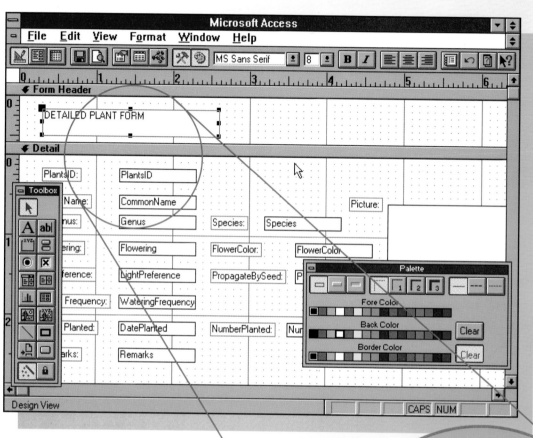

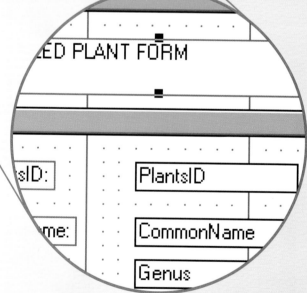

"Why would I do this?"

You can use a label box to give your form a more professional appearance, and make it easier to use by adding text as a title or other information that helps the usability of your form. For example, if you are not the only person who is using this form, you can add a small label box of instructions concerning the form and the information required for it. This can help someone who is new to your form get a good start without you having to watch them.

In this task, you learn to add a form title in a label box.

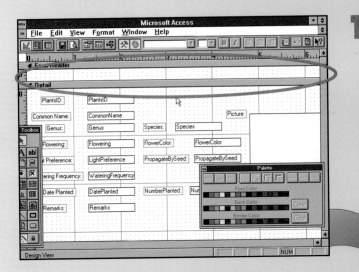

1 Select **Format** from the menu, and choose **Form Header/Footer** from the drop-down menu. You now see a new blank area above the detail form area. This is the Form Header area. This section prints and is displayed at the top of each form. If you use the scroll bar on the right of your screen and scroll down, you see a corresponding Form Footer area. This section appears at the bottom of each form.

2 Click the **Label Box** button on the toolbox.

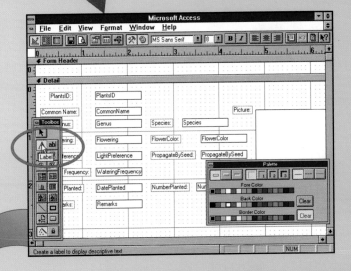

3 Move the pointer to the Form Header area. You see that the pointer has again changed shape. Position the crosshairs, or plus sign, where you want to begin your label box.

Task 32: Creating a Label Box

4 Drag diagonally across the opposite corner of the box and release the mouse button.

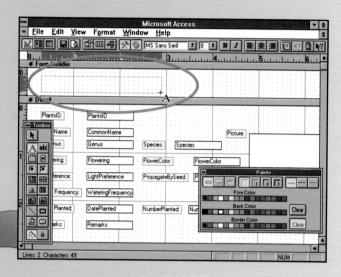

5 When you release the mouse button you see the flashing cursor inside the label box. Type **DETAILED PLANT FORM** as the title for this form, and then press the **Enter** key to select the label box again.

WHY WORRY?

If you decide that you do not want to keep this label box, simply select it and press the Delete key. If your text does not fit within the label box, just select the box and then drag the resize handles to enlarge the box.

6 You can add color to your label box and other form objects by using the color bars in the Palette toolbar. Turn on the Palette by choosing it from the View menu. Select the label box to be modified. Change the text color by clicking a color on the Fore Color toolbar. Select a color for the label box by selecting a color from the Back Color toolbar. Choose a color from the Border Color toolbar to change the color of the label boxes' border.

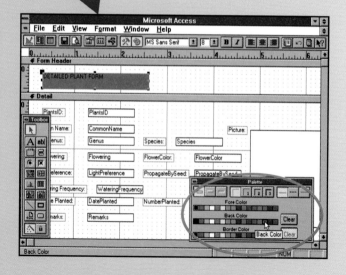

Adding a List Box

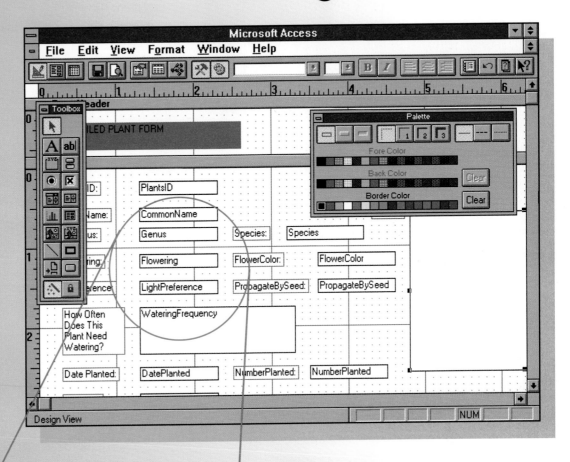

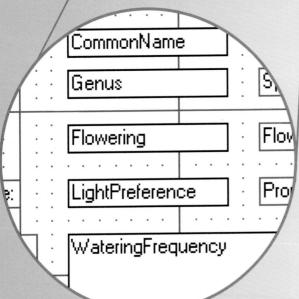

"Why would I do this?"

You can use a list box to restrict the information in a field to a list of preselected choices. This capability can help later when you create reports and give simple consistency to your database. Using a list box to fill in selected information also ensures that your table remains accurate, that you have not misspelled data, and that your information always contains one of several responses.

In this task, you learn to remove a field from the form and replace it with a list of options.

Task 33: Adding a List Box

1 Select the field WateringFrequency on your form. Remember, select a field by clicking the right box on the right side.

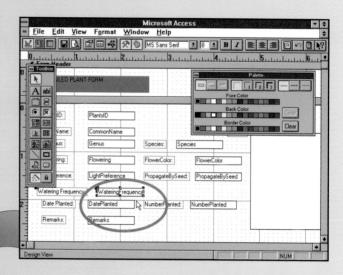

2 Press the **Delete** key. Access for Windows removes this field from your form. This field has only been removed from the form, not deleted from your table.

3 Click the **Control Wizards** button on the second toolbar, and then the **List Box** button. Notice how these buttons now seem to be depressed on the toolbar. This indicates that they are selected for use.

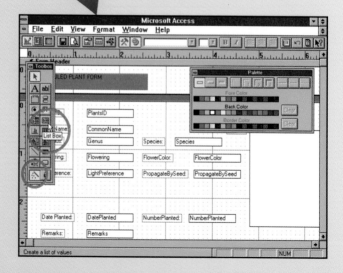

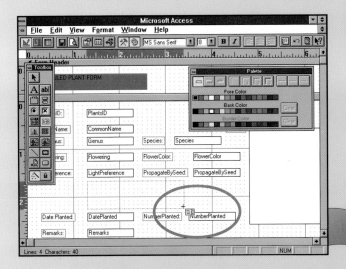

4 Move the mouse pointer to the location where you want to place the list box, and drag the pointer to the opposite corner of your list box. Notice that the mouse pointer has changed into a plus sign with a list box attached.

NOTE ▼

Be sure to leave room for your field. You need at least enough room for your list box to display a scroll bar if needed. Access for Windows adds an up and down scroll bar so that you can view all the options available.

5 Click the second radio button option in the List Box Wizard dialog box now displayed. Click the **Next >** button to display the next dialog box.

NOTE ▼

The first option allows you to enter the options displayed in the list in another table. This choice is good if the options that you want to display in this list are updated and changed fairly often. You can also use the results of a query for your list of options.

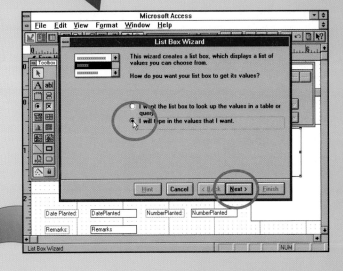

6 Type a **1** in the text box Number of columns, and then click the mouse pointer in the columns box below the text box. This box changes to display only the single column that you want. You can create a list that includes more than one column in it.

Task 33: Adding a List Box

7 Type **Keep Wet** in the first row of Col1. Press the **down-arrow** key once to move the cursor to the next field. Type **Keep Moist** and press the **down-arrow** key again. In the next three rows type: **Dry Out Between Watering**, **Weekly**, **Keep Dry**. Be sure to press the **down-arrow** key between each entry. Click the **Next >** button to display the next dialog box.

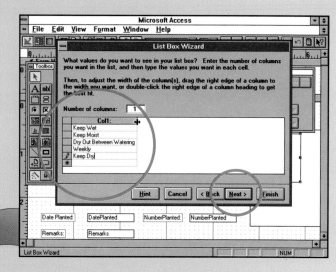

8 Click the second radio button and then the **down-arrow** button beside the text box. Select the field name WateringFrequency from the drop-down list box. This tells Access for Windows to store your selection from the list in the Watering-Frequency field in your table. Click the **Next >** button to display the next dialog box.

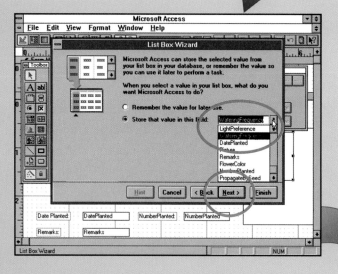

9 You use this dialog box to enter a label for your field.

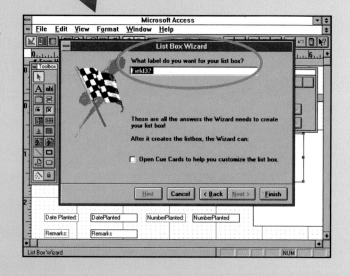

118

10 Type **How Often Does This Plant Need Watering?** as the label for this field. There is no reason that you can't use a label to tell you what kind of information is needed or why you may need it. Click the **Finish** button.

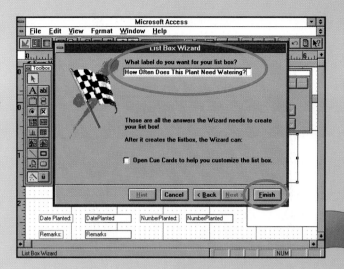

11 You see the field name WateringFrequency displayed in the field box. You also notice that the label that you entered for this field does not fit in the label box for this field.

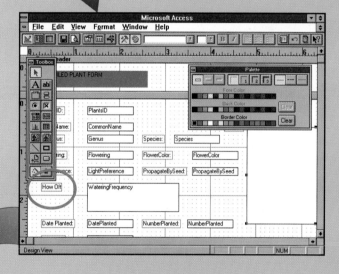

12 Click the label box to select it. Drag the bottom right corner to enlarge the label box. You can now see the entire label, and the label box is more in proportion to the size of the list box.

WHY WORRY?

As with all other fields, you can delete a list box. As you use the List Wizard, click the < Back button to go to a previous dialog box and make a correction.

TASK 34

Changing a Label

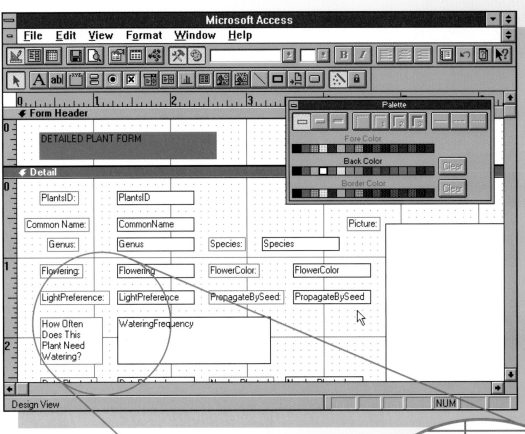

"Why would I do this?"

If you find that a field name does not adequately describe the information that you enter into a field, you can change the field's label on your form. Use the field label to remind yourself what type of information is supposed to be entered or why the information is needed. Sometimes using labels in the form of a question can help you to fill in a form.

In this task, you learn to change an existing field label.

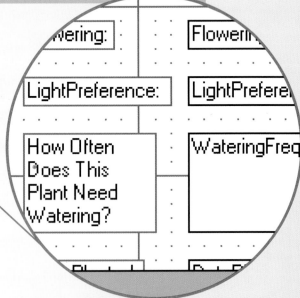

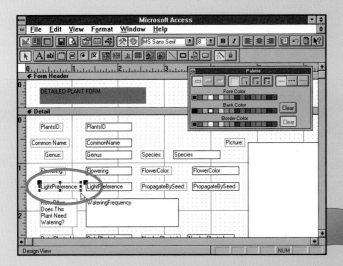

1 Select the field label **LightPreference**. You now see the resizing handles surrounding the field label box, and the movement handle displayed on the field LightPreference.

2 Click the mouse pointer inside the field label box. The blinking cursor is displayed inside the label box. Press the **Backspace** or **Delete** key, and delete all the text. Type **What Kind Of Light Does This Plant Prefer?** Notice how the label box expands to include all the new text, and that it has now overflowed over the field box.

WHY WORRY?

You can change the field label text at any time. If you find that a label is confusing, change it.

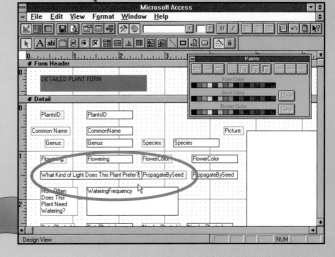

3 Click the label box again to display the resize and movement handles. Drag the field box's move handle to the right until the field box is no longer behind the field label box.

NOTE ▼

To change the appearance of a field or label, select a button. Choose either the Raised or Sunken Appearance buttons on the palette. To change back, click the Normal Appearance button.

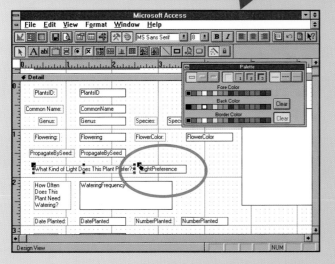

TASK 35

Using a Combo Box

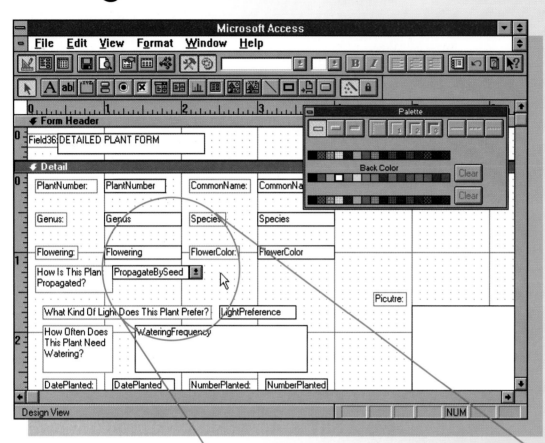

"Why would I do this?"

A combination box, also called a combo box, is a good option if you do not have enough space for a list box or if you do not want to display more than the selected option on your form. A list box displays a drop-down list with your available options.

In this task, you learn to add a combo box to your form.

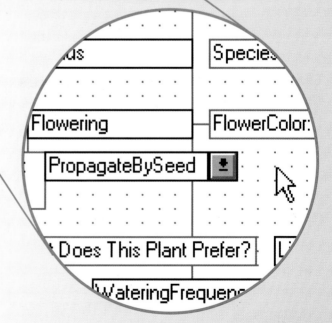

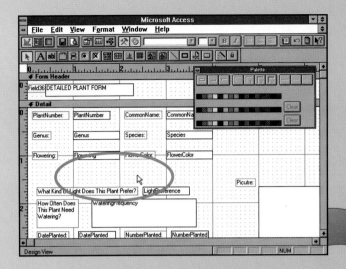

1 Select the field PropagateBySeed and press the **Delete** key to delete this field from the form.

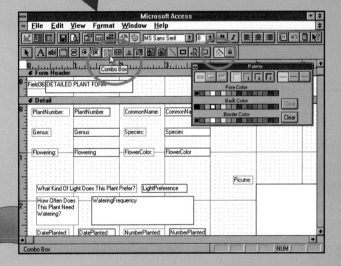

2 Click the **Control Wizard** button, and then the **Combo Box** button.

3 Move the mouse pointer to the form where you want to place the Combo box. Click and drag across to create your list box.

4 Click the second radio button in the Combo Box Wizard dialog box. This allows you to enter the options that are available for selection. Click the **Next >** button to display the next dialog box.

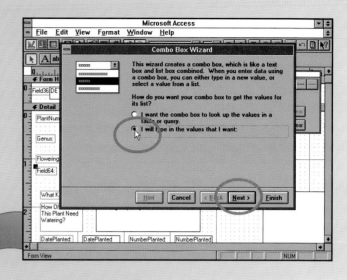

5 Select the number of columns that you need for your combination box. Type the number **1** in the text box, and then click the mouse pointer in the column area. You see the number of columns change from 2 to 1.

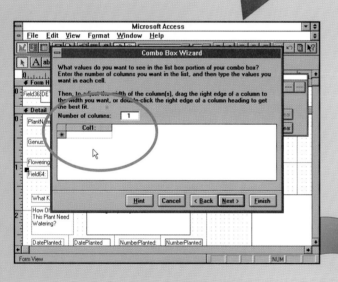

6 Type **Seeds** in the first row of Col1. Press the **down-arrow** key to move the cursor to the next row. Type **Tubers** and press the **down-arrow** key again to move to the next row. Type **Bulbs**, **Corms**, **Rhizomes**, **Cuttings**, and **Divisions** pressing the **down-arrow** key between each entry. Click the **Next >** button to display the next dialog box.

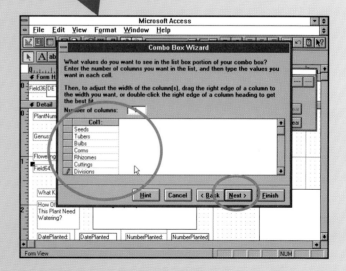

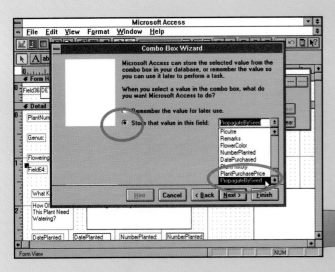

7 Click the second radio button to store your selected option in your table. Then click the **down-arrow** button beside the text box, and select the field name PropagateBySeed from the drop-down list. Click the **Next >** button to display the next dialog box.

8 Type **How Is This Plant Propagated?** in the text box for the label to be displayed for this field on your form. Click the **Finish** button.

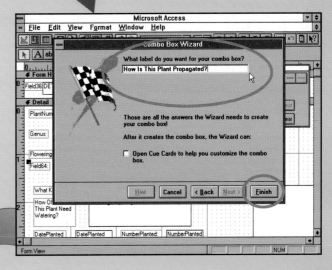

9 Resize the field label box to display the new label.

WHY WORRY?

You always can add to your options list later if you find that you have not included all the options that you need.

125

Drawing Lines and Rectangles

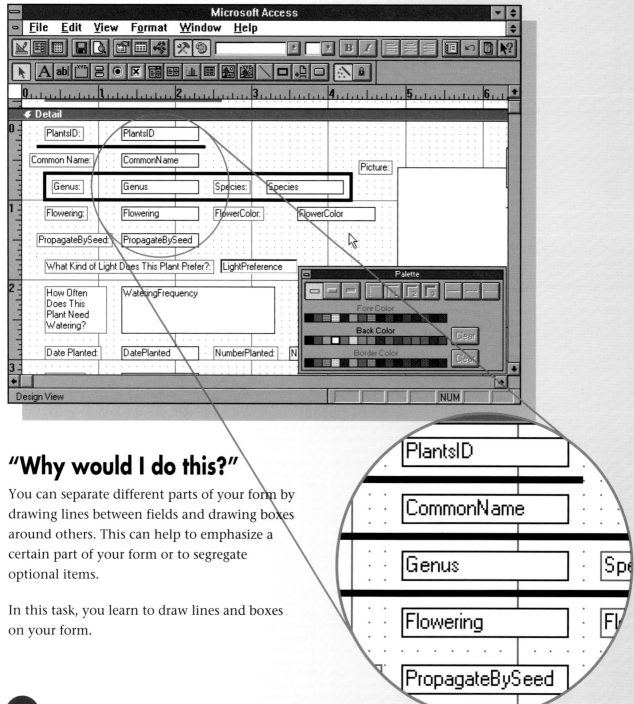

"Why would I do this?"

You can separate different parts of your form by drawing lines between fields and drawing boxes around others. This can help to emphasize a certain part of your form or to segregate optional items.

In this task, you learn to draw lines and boxes on your form.

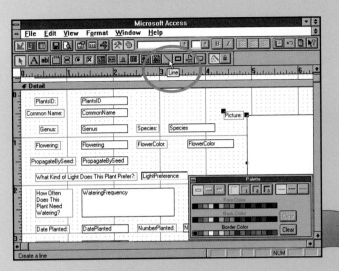

1 Move the cursor to the second toolbar and click the **Line** button.

2 Move the mouse pointer to the form window. You see the pointer has again changed shape to a crosshair with a dangling line. Place the pointer underneath the field label PlantsID and click and drag the pointer to the 2-inch mark on the horizontal ruler.

NOTE ▼

Just like a label or field box, you can move and resize a line by dragging the resize handles. You can draw a line at an angle or vertically, by dragging a resize handle up or down.

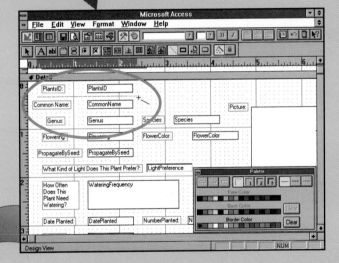

3 Click the **3-pt. Border Width** button on the Palette floating toolbar. You see your line become heavier or thicker. You can choose between a Hairline Border, 1-pt. Border, 2-pt. Border, and the 3-pt. Border.

4 Move the pointer to the second toolbar, and click the **Rectangle** button.

> **NOTE** ▼
>
> You can change the thickness of your rectangle's borders just as you did the line.

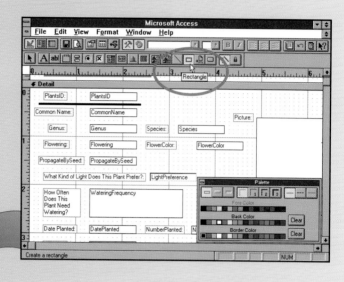

5 Move the pointer back to the form and drag a rectangle around the field labels and fields for both Genus and Species.

> **WHY WORRY?**
>
> Lines and rectangles, or boxes, can be deleted or resized at any time. You can also change the thickness of the lines from Hairline to 3-point as you choose.

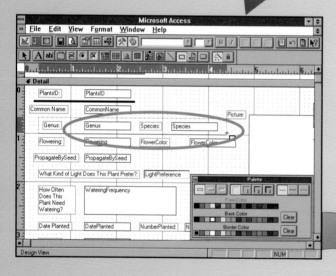

6 Release the mouse pointer. You now seem to have lost your two fields. They are simply beneath the box that you have just drawn. Click the top **Clear** button on the Palette toolbar beside the color bar labeled Back Color. This makes the inside of the box transparent so that you are able to see your fields beneath it. This does not affect the borders of your rectangle.

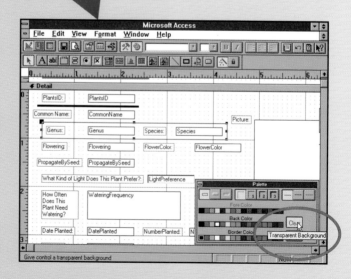

Adding Toggle Buttons

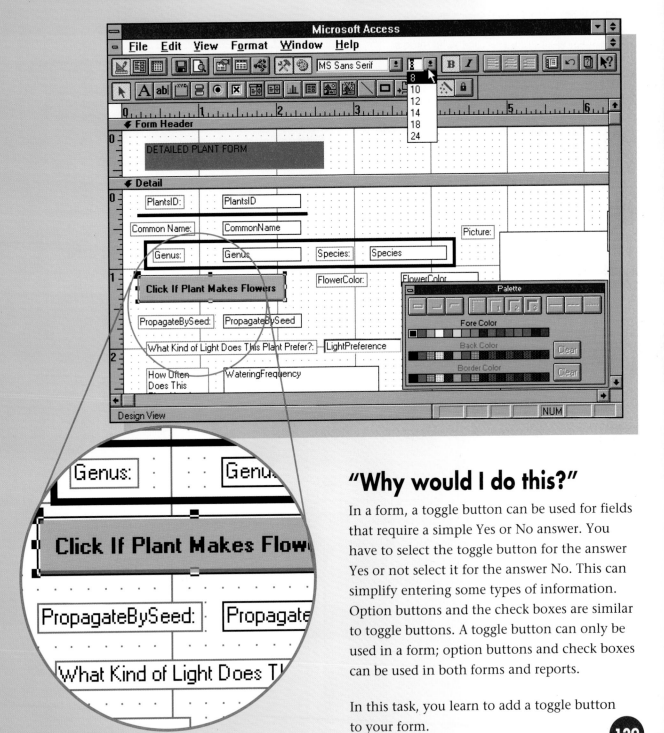

"Why would I do this?"

In a form, a toggle button can be used for fields that require a simple Yes or No answer. You have to select the toggle button for the answer Yes or not select it for the answer No. This can simplify entering some types of information. Option buttons and the check boxes are similar to toggle buttons. A toggle button can only be used in a form; option buttons and check boxes can be used in both forms and reports.

In this task, you learn to add a toggle button to your form.

Task 37: Adding Toggle Buttons

1 Delete the field Flowering, and then click
the **Control Wizards** button and then
the **Toggle Button** button. You now see
a blank button displayed.

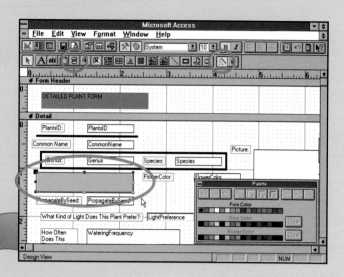

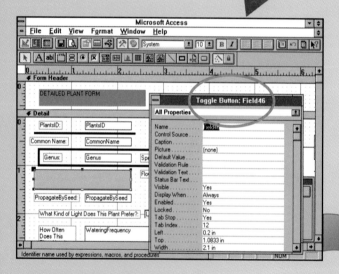

2 Click the form to deselect the blank button
and remove the resize handles. Now move
the mouse pointer back to the toggle
button and double-click on it. You now see
the Toggle Button properties dialog box.

3 Click the mouse pointer in the box labeled
Control source and then on the **down-
arrow** button that is displayed. Select the
field name Flowering from the list. This
binds this field to the toggle button.

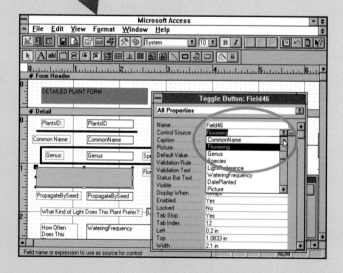

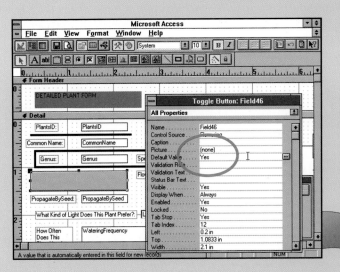

4 Press the **down-arrow** key three times to the Default Value box, and type **Yes**.

5 Double-click the Control menu button to close the Toggle Button properties dialog box. Move the mouse pointer to the button face and click once.

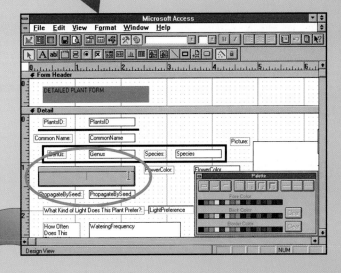

6 Type **Click If Plant Makes Flowers**. Click outside the toggle button to place the label on the button face.

7 As you can see, the text does not quite fit on the toggle button face. Select the button again by clicking it. Notice how the Font Name and Font Size text boxes on the first toolbar are now filled in. Select a different font by clicking the **down-arrow** button beside the Font Name text box. Select a new font from the list of available fonts. As soon as you select the new font, the text on the button face changes to the selected font.

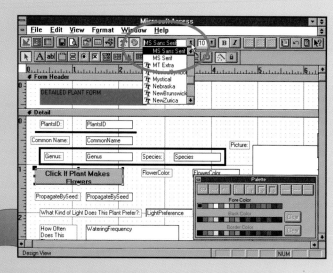

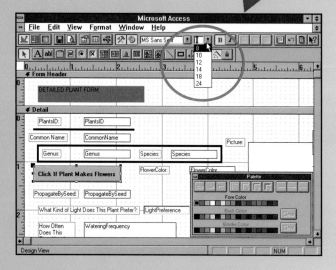

8 Click the **down-arrow** button beside the Font Size text box to change the size of the font of the selected button or text box. Select a font size of **8** from the list. You now see that the text fits quite well on the button's face.

WHY WORRY?

If the text you enter does not fit on your toggle button, you can enlarge the button, change the label so that it is smaller, change the font size, or any combination of these.

Saving Your New Form

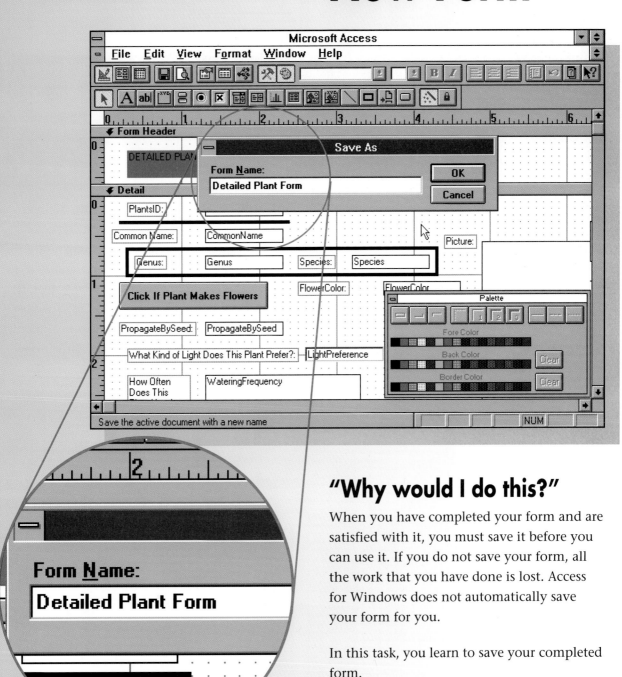

"Why would I do this?"

When you have completed your form and are satisfied with it, you must save it before you can use it. If you do not save your form, all the work that you have done is lost. Access for Windows does not automatically save your form for you.

In this task, you learn to save your completed form.

Task 38: Saving Your New Form

1 Click the **Save** button on the first toolbar. Selecting this button tells Access for Windows that you want to save your form.

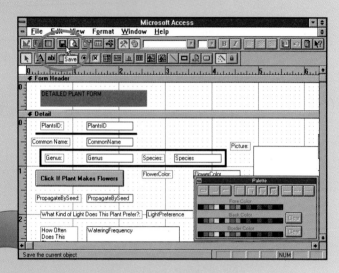

2 Enter a name for this form into the text box of the Save As dialog box. Type **Detailed Plant Form**. Remember to use a name that easily jogs your memory as to the function of this report. Click the **OK** button in the Save As dialog box to save this form. Double-click the Control menu button to close the Form Design window.

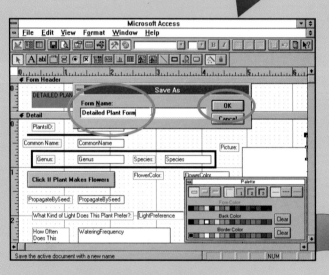

3 You now see your new form listed in the forms list of the Database window.

WHY WORRY?

Remember, you can always delete a form and create it again if you find that it does not fit your needs.

Opening a Form

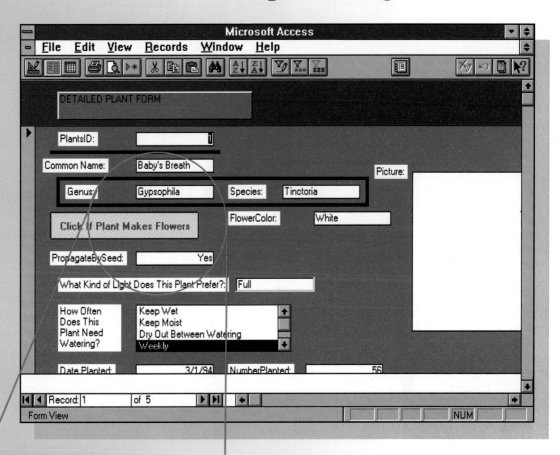

"Why would I do this?"

You must open your form before you can enter or edit information through the form. Remember, the form is simply another way to look at the information contained in your table.

In this task, you learn to open your form.

Task 39: Opening a Form

1 From the Database window, click the **Form** button. This displays the list of available forms that you have created to use with your database.

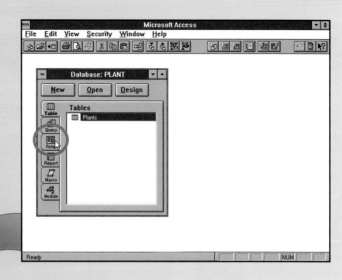

2 Click on the form name in the list. This highlights the name. You can also use the up- or down-arrow keys to move the highlighted block from form name to form name.

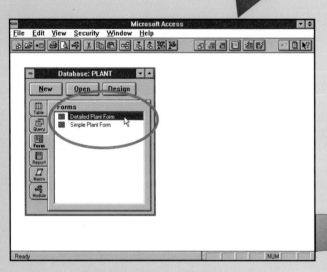

3 Click the **Open** button above the form name list box. You now see your form displayed on-screen. To see more of your form on-screen, click the **Maximize** button—the small upward facing triangle button located at the upper right corner of the form window.

Entering and Editing Information in a Form

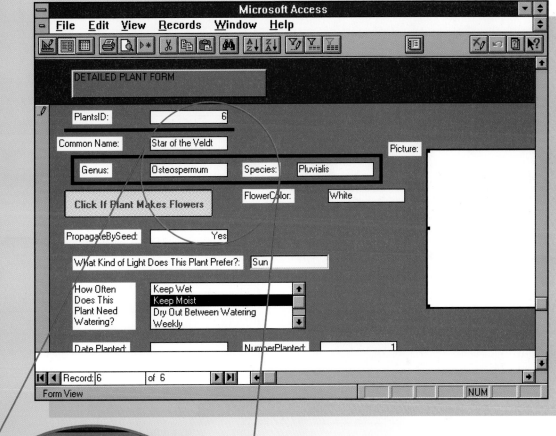

"Why would I do this?"

Using a form to enter new information and to edit old information is more familiar (for most people) than using a table. When you are more familiar with a format, you are less likely to make mistakes.

In this task, you learn to enter and edit information by using the form.

Task 40: Entering and Editing Information in a Form

1 To enter new information in a table, you must get to the next new record line. When using a form, you can't see the last record like you can when using a table. To quickly get to the last record of the table in a form, click the **Go to last record** button just above the status line on your screen. You now see the last record in your table.

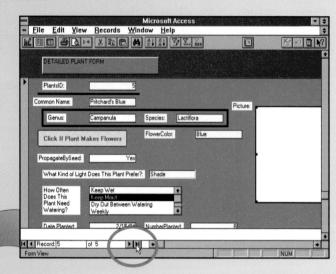

2 Click the **Next record** button, which is located to the left of the **Go to last record** button. You now see a blank form on your screen.

NOTE ▼

If you have not placed your fields on your form in the same order that they occur in your table, you notice that the cursor appears to jump around your form. It is simply following the order that the fields are added to your table.

3 Press the **Enter** key to move to the first field CommonName and type **Star Of The Veldt**. Press the **Enter** key to move to the next field. Type **Osteospermum** for Genus, **Pluvialis** for Species, and **White** for FlowerColor.

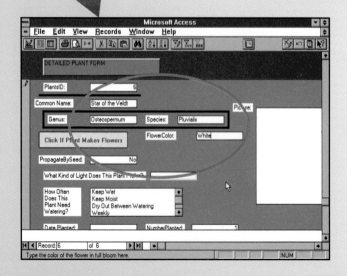

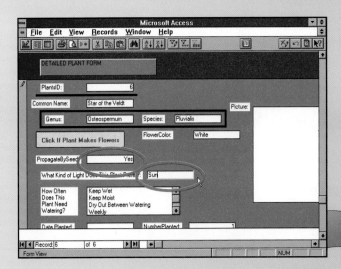

4 Type **Yes** in the PropagateBySeed field and **Sun** in the What Kind of Light Does This Plant Prefer? field.

5 Select the correct option for the field How Often Does This Plant Need Watering? by clicking the choice that you want to select. If you do not see the option, use the scroll bar to display additional options.

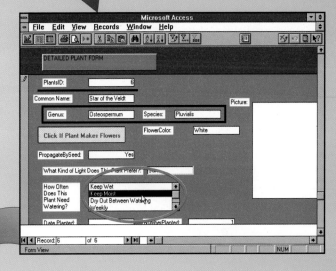

6 Exit from the form by pressing **Ctrl+F4**. You are returned to the Database window.

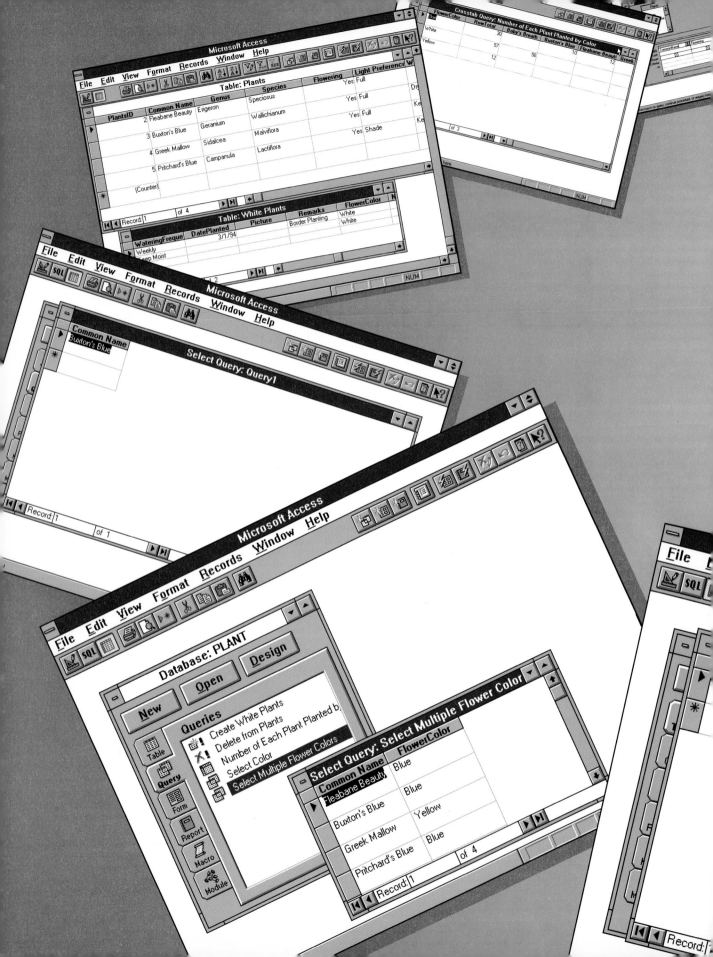

PART V

Getting Information from a Database

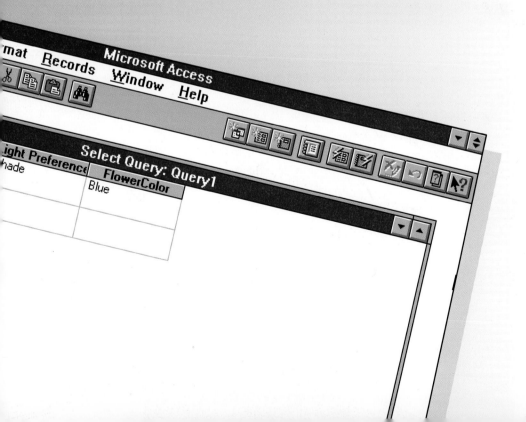

Part V: Getting Information from a Database

In the last several parts of this book, you learned to design and build a table to store information, create a form that you can use to display and enter information, and enter and edit data. Gathering and storing information in an organized fashion is all well and good, but those tasks are only half the reason for collecting data. In addition to collecting and storing information, you must be able to find and make use of that information.

You can ask Access for Windows questions about your information. A question is called a *query*. Unlike a simple card file, which is another way to collect and organize information, Access for Windows can respond to a query to find all records that meet certain criteria. *Criteria* simply are restrictions on the information to be included. For example, you can query Access for Windows to find the records of all your customers who live in Oregon; the criterion is that a record must include *Oregon* in the state field.

Showing customers from a specified state is a simple query. You also can create complex queries, such as "Show me the records of all customers who bought items A, B, and C more than twice in the past year" or "Create a list of customers who do *not* live in New York." Queries like these can help you focus your attention on specific details of your business.

Criteria can include more than one field or table. For example, you could construct a query that finds all customers who live in California or New York and who have bought more than $500 worth of merchandise in the past year.

Some of the tasks for which you can use a query are:

- Showing records that meet specified criteria

- Displaying information from a table in a different order from that used in the table

- Updating records that meet certain criteria

- Displaying selected information from several tables at once

- Adding information from one table to another

- Deleting selected information from a table

You can create several different types of queries, each of which produces a different result. The most commonly used are:

Select query. This type of query enables you to specify various criteria for Access for Windows to use in selecting records. All the selected records then are displayed in a new table called the *dynaset*.

Crosstab query. This type of query is often used to graph information from a table. You can create a crosstab query to display trends and to generate summaries of your information. There is a Wizard to help create this type of query.

Action query. This type of query is used to add information to, or edit information in, a group of records in a table. For example, you can use an action query to update the prices of items that you sell. You also can use an action query to add records, delete records, or create a new table.

After you create a query, you can use the resulting answer, or dynaset, in a form or report. You can create a query that uses information from several tables. For example, you could combine information from a Sales table and a Customer table to find out who your best customers are. Basing a query on a report ensures that the report has the most up-to-date information. You easily can create a query that selects all customers who have past-due invoices. Then you can use the resulting dynaset to create a report that lists these customers, their phone numbers, the invoices that are past due, and the total past-due amount.

When you begin to create queries, write down your questions. The simple task of putting a question on paper helps you focus on what you are looking for, and also helps you revise a query if you don't get the answer or format you were expecting. Be as specific as possible in building your query statement, and then refine it if necessary. The more specific you are when you write your question, the easier the job of putting together the actual query will be.

Creating a Select Query

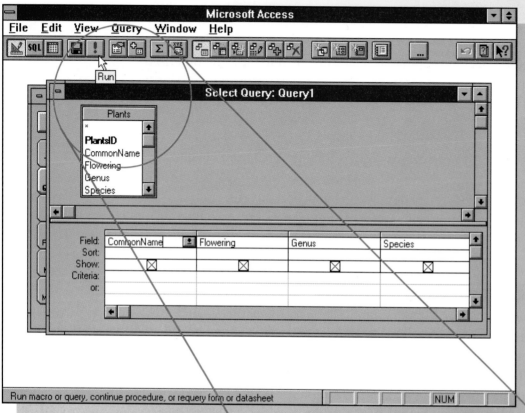

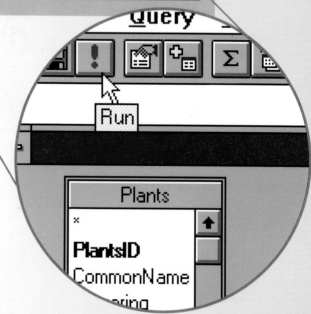

"Why would I do this?"

Select queries are the most common type of query. When you use a select query, Access for Windows selects and displays records that meet the criteria you entered. For example, you could create a query that says, "Display all records for plants that have white flowers, and include only the CommonName, Genus, Species, and NumberPlanted fields."

In this task, you create and use a select query.

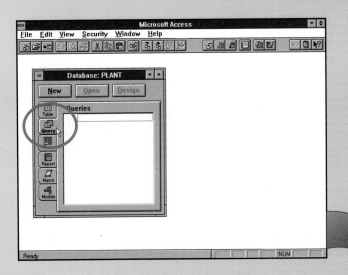

1 Open your database file. In the Database window, click the **Query** button. You see a blank Query list. After you create and save a query, the query appears in this list.

> **NOTE** ▼
>
> Access for Windows automatically assumes that you want to base your query on a table. If you plan to base a query on the result of another query, you need to click one of the radio buttons—Queries or Both—at the bottom of the dialog box.

2 Click the **New** button in the Database window. You now see the New Query dialog box. Click the **New Query** button in this dialog box. You see the Add Table dialog box and the Select Query window. Click **Add** to add the Plants table to the Select Query window, and then click **Close** to close the Add Table dialog box.

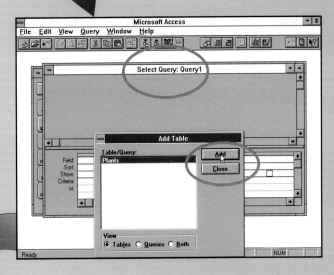

3 If you had more than one table in your database, each table would be listed in this dialog box, and you would have had to select the tables to be included and then add each one to the Select Query window.

4 In the table list box, select the first field to be included in your query by double-clicking the field **CommonName**. Access places that field in the first column of the query grid. Select all your fields this way; Access puts each one in the next available column.

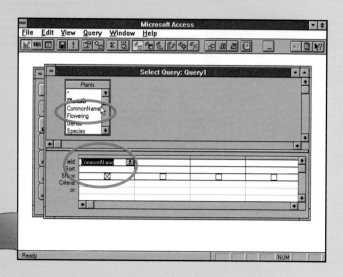

NOTE ▼

To include all fields in the query, double-click the asterisk (*) above the other field names. Access enters each field, listing the fields as a group that prints in the same order as in your table.

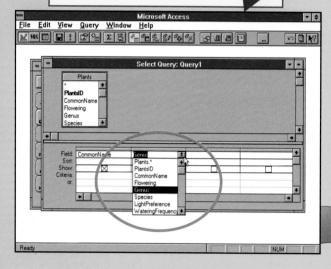

5 Click the field row of the second column. Then click the **down-arrow** button that now appears at the end of the field. You see a drop-down list of field names from the selected table. Click **Genus** to include it as the second field. Use this step to include the Species and NumberPlanted fields in the third and fourth columns.

WHY WORRY?

If you include a column that you don't want, click the bar at the top of the column and press Del.

6 Scroll through the list until you find FlowerColor, and then double-click it. Nothing happens on-screen. Now click the **right-arrow** button in the bottom scroll bar. You see the FlowerColor field, which you added.

NOTE ▼

To make the Query window bigger, expand the Select Query window by clicking the Maximize button or by clicking and dragging the sides of the window.

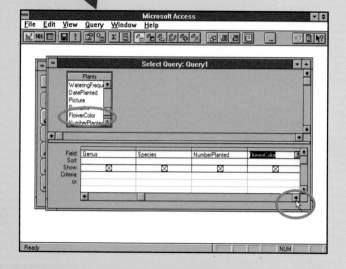

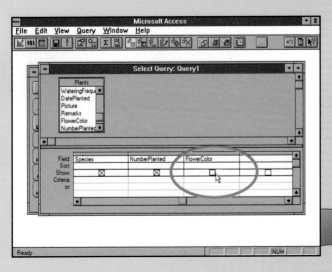

7 Click the **Show** box in the column that contains the FlowerColor field name. The click removes the X, indicating that this field will be used in the selection criteria but will not be displayed in the answer dynaset.

8 Click the row **Criteria** in the FlowerColor column, and then type **"White"**. This step specifies the criterion that selected records must meet—they must have white flowers.

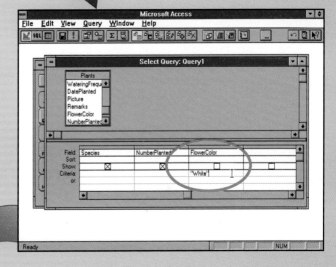

9 In the toolbar, click the **Run** button. Access for Windows runs your query.

Task 41: Creating a Select Query

10 The answer dynaset appears on-screen. This select query found the plants that you sought.

WHY WORRY?

If you find that your query did not work as you expected, go back to the Database window, select it in the Query list, and then choose the Design button. You then can make any necessary changes and try again.

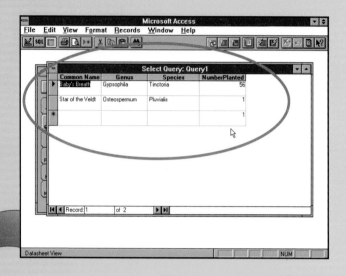

11 Select **File** from the menu bar, and then choose the **Save Query As** option from the drop-down menu.

12 Type **Select Color** in the text box of the Save As dialog box, and then click the **OK** button. Access for Windows saves the query with this name. You can easily use this select query again when you need it. Close the query.

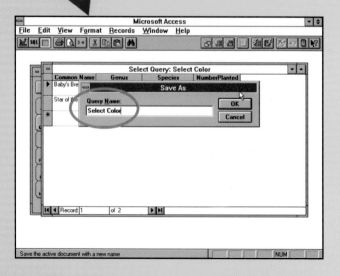

Using a Crosstab Query

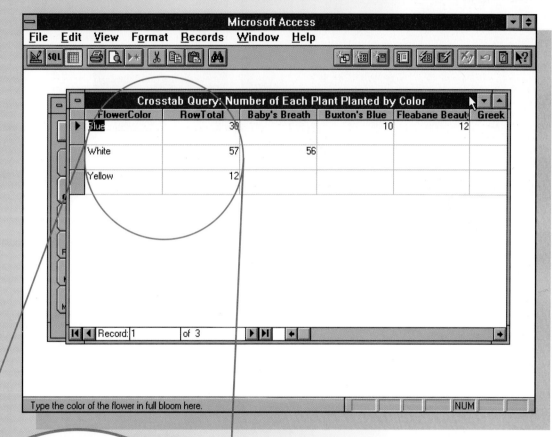

"Why would I do this?"

One key to succeeding in business is being able to spot trends and analyze information. Although an Access for Windows table is an efficient method of collecting information, it is not always the best way to use your information for other purposes. A crosstab query can help you distill trends and analyze the information that you collect by comparing one field of information with another field.

In this task, you create a crosstab query. You use the Plants table to answer the query, "How many plants of each color do I have?"

149

Task 42: Using a Crosstab Query

1 Open the Database window and click the **Query** button. Then click the **New** button at the top of the Database window. The New Query dialog box appears.

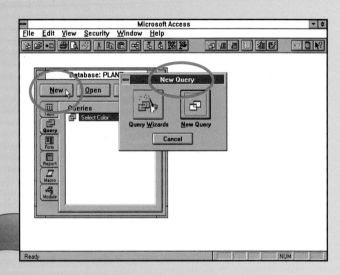

2 Click the **Query Wizards** button. You see the dialog box that you will use to select a Query Wizard. Select the option **Crosstab Query**.

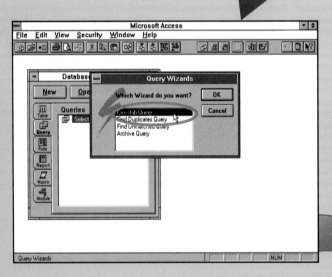

3 Click the **OK** button to open the Crosstab Query Wizard dialog box. Access for Windows selects the **Tables** option by default. If you want to base this query on the result of another query, choose the **Queries** option; to use both tables and queries, choose the **Both** option.

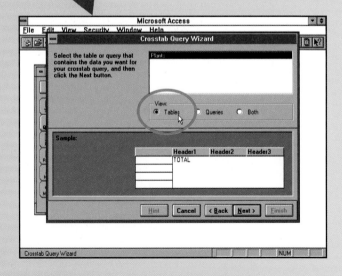

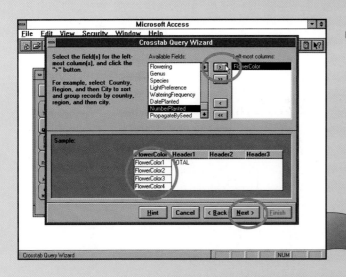

4 Click the **Next >** button to open the next Crosstab Query Wizard dialog box. Click the field **FlowerColor**, and then click the > button. This action moves the field name from the Available Fields list to the Left-most columns list. As you see from the sample in the dialog box, Access for Windows uses the selected field as the first field.

5 Click the **Next >** button to open the next Crosstab Query Wizard dialog box. Then click the field name **CommonName** in the list at the top of this dialog box. Access for Windows will use the entries in this field as headings for the remaining columns.

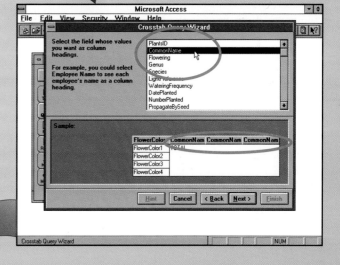

NOTE ▼

Notice that the field you used for the first column—FlowerColor—does not appear in this list. You are not allowed to compare something with itself.

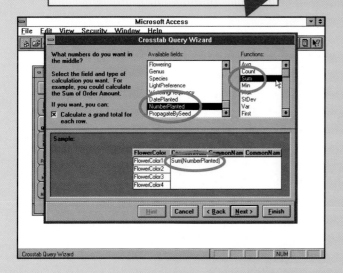

6 Click the **Next >** button to open the next Crosstab Query Wizard dialog box. Select the field name **NumberPlanted** in the Available fields list. Then click **Sum** in the Functions list. This action tells Access to add all plants with the same name and color, and enter the number of planted plants of each common name and each color.

7 Click the **Next** button again. Type **Number of Each Plant Planted by Color** as the name of this query.

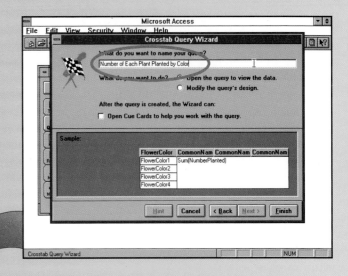

8 Click the **Finish** button. Access for Windows creates and displays the result of this query and saves the query in the Query list.

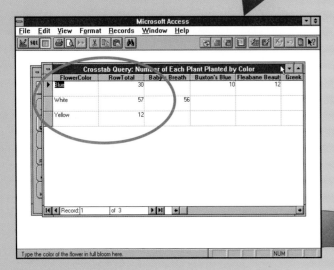

9 Press **Ctrl+F4** to close the Crosstab Query dynaset table, and then click the **Yes** button to save any changes you made.

WHY WORRY?

If your query does not display the information that you expected or in the format that you needed, look at your original query statement. Go over each step that you made when you created the query, and make any necessary changes. Then run the query again.

TASK 43

Creating an Action Query

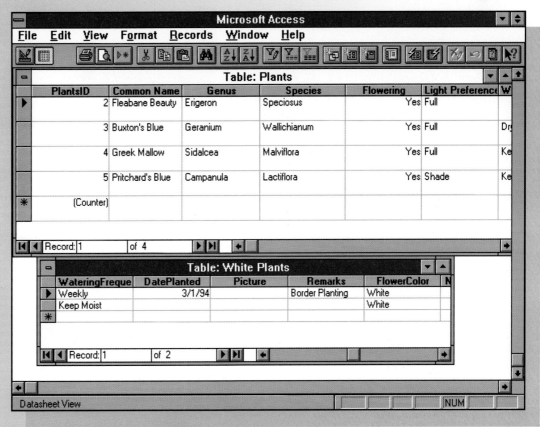

"Why would I do this?"

Use an action query when you need to make large, repetitive changes in a table, for example. If you want to increase the prices of your products by 10 percent, use an action query. You can create an action query to perform the same action in a selected record or in a table.

In this task, you create an action query that selects specified records, deletes them from the Plants table, and adds them to another table. This type of query also is called an *archive query*.

Task 43: Creating an Action Query

1 Open the Database window, and then click the **Query** button to open the Query list. Now click the **New** button, and then click the **Query Wizards** button in the New Query dialog box.

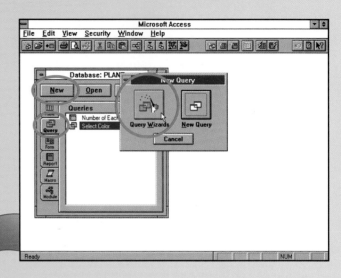

2 Select the option **Archive Query** in the list of Wizards, and then click the **OK** button.

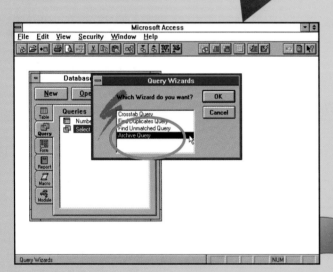

3 Select the table or tables to be included in your query. (Because you have only one table—Plants—only that table appears in the list.) Click the **Next >** button.

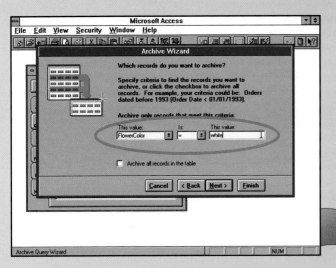

4 Click the **down-arrow** button beside the first This value text box. Select the field **FlowerColor**. Click the **down-arrow** button beside the Is text box, and select the operator **=** (equal sign). Then type **white** in the second This value text box.

5 Click the **Next >** button. You see the next Archive Wizard dialog box. This box shows the records selected by the query statement that you created in the preceding dialog box. By using the scroll bar, you can scroll these records across the screen to verify that they are plants with white flowers.

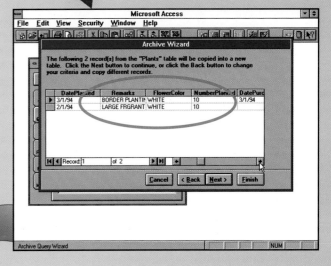

6 Click the **Next >** button again. In the next Archive Wizard dialog box that appears, you can choose to delete the records from the original table or to leave them there and simply copy them to the new table. Click the first option button, **Yes, I want to delete the original record(s)**.

7 Click the **Next >** button to display the next Archive Wizard dialog box. In the text box, type **White Plants** as the name for this archive table. Click the **Finish** button to save the query and table.

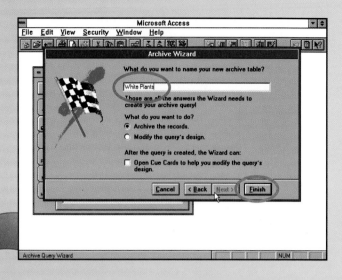

8 You now see a dialog box asking you to confirm that you want to copy records from one table to another table. Click the **Yes** button. You see another dialog box, asking whether you want to delete the records from the first table. Click the **Yes** button in this box to delete the records, and then click the **OK** button in the last dialog box, which tells you that the job is complete.

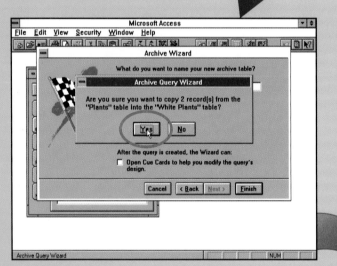

9 Click the **Table** button to display the table list. You now see two tables listed: Plants and White Plants. There were also two new queries created: White Plants and Delete White Plants.

WHY WORRY?

If you use an archive query to delete records, you will always have a copy of the deleted records, and those records will be available if you ever need to use them.

Choosing Records Using Wild Cards

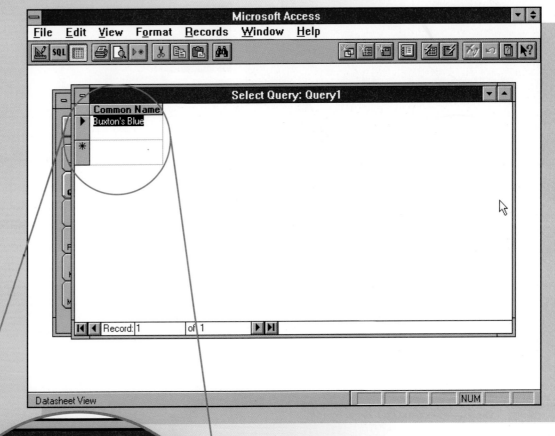

"Why would I do this?"

You can use *wild-card* characters to find words that contain certain letters, or patterns of letters. The most common wild-card characters are the question mark (?) and the asterisk (*). A question mark represents any single character; an asterisk represents any number of characters beginning from the point where you place the asterisk.

In this task, you use wild-card characters in a select query to find all plants with a common name beginning with the letter *B*.

157

Task 44: Choosing Records Using Wild Cards

1 Open the Database window, and click the **Query** button. Then click the **New** button. Now click the **New Query** button in the New Query dialog box. You see the Add Table dialog box and the Select Query window behind it.

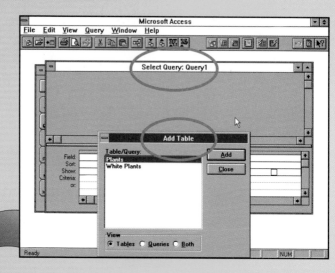

2 Select **Plants** from the list in the Add Table dialog box, and click the **Add** button. You see the Plants field-name list displayed at the top of the Select Query window. Click the **Close** button in the Add Table dialog box to remove it from view.

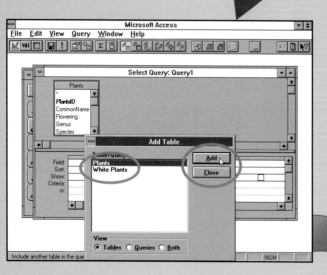

3 Double-click the field **CommonName** in the Plants field-name list. Click in the Criteria row of the query grid by pressing the **down-arrow** key three times.

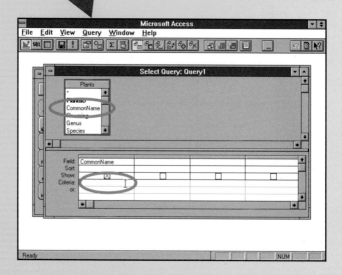

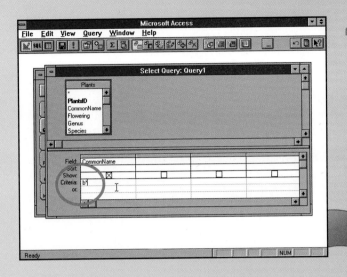

4 Type **b***. This entry tells Access to search for and then display all the plants whose names begin with the letter *B*. Press the **down-arrow** key again. Notice that Access has changed your criterion to read Like "B*".

NOTE ▼

When using a wild-card character in a query, you do not have to be case-specific. Access considers an uppercase *B* to be the same as a lowercase *b*.

5 Click the **Run** button in the toolbar. Access for Windows displays the result of your query. As you can see, all the plants with a common name beginning with the letter *B* are displayed.

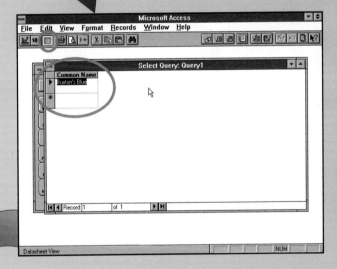

6 Close the window containing the answer dynaset by double-clicking the **Control menu** button and then clicking the **No** button in the dialog box that appears.

WHY WORRY?

If you don't find the information that you are seeking, look at your query statement again.

Selecting Records that Match Criteria

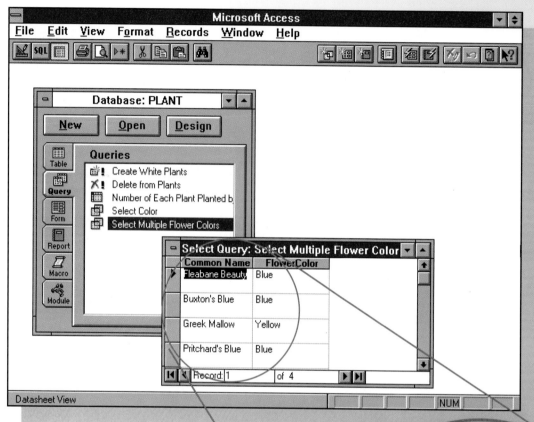

"Why would I do this?"

Sometimes, you want to find records that meet one or another criterion. If you want to find all plants that have yellow or blue flowers, you can create a query that will find these plants. A query that says "Select this or that" uses an *OR* operator, which tells Access to select any record that meets one criterion or the other. A selected record does not have to meet both criteria. In this task, you use the OR operator in a query that displays all plants that have yellow or blue flowers.

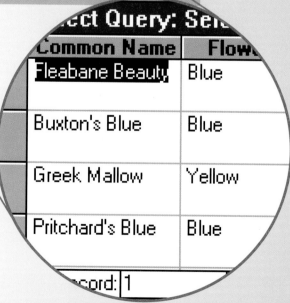

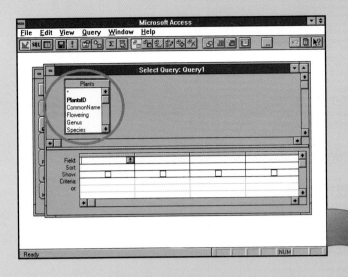

1 From the Query list in the Database window, click the **New** button, and then click the **New Query** button in the New Query dialog box. In the Add Table dialog box, select the **Plants** table and click the **Add** button. The Plants field-name list appears at the top of the Select Query window. Click the **Close** button in the Add Table dialog box to remove it from view.

2 Select, by double-clicking, the field **CommonName** in the Plants list.

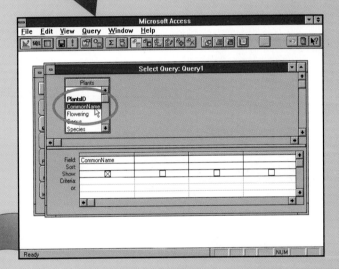

3 Scroll down the Plants list, and double-click **FlowerColor** to add that field to the Query grid.

4 Click in the Criteria row of the FlowerColor column. Type **"yellow" Or "blue"** and press the **down-arrow** key.

NOTE ▼

You also can enter this criterion in two rows. Notice that the row below the Criteria row is called OR. You can enter the first criterion (yellow) in the Criteria row and then enter the second criterion (blue) in the or row.

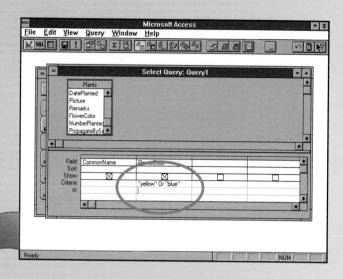

5 Double-click the **Control menu** button in the Select Query window. Click the **Yes** button to save your query. Type **Select Multiple Flower Colors** in the text box of the Save As dialog box. Click **OK**.

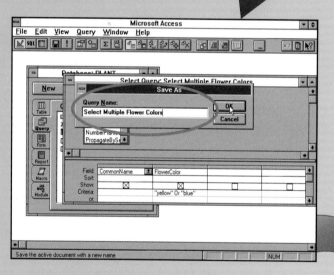

6 Click the query **Select Multiple Flower Colors** to select it, and then click the **Open** button.

WHY WORRY?

If your query does not find records that meet the criteria you entered, make sure that you did not misspell your criteria (for example, yello instead of yellow). Also, the criterion Yellow will not find Yellow Tones, but Yellow* will find Yellow Tones.

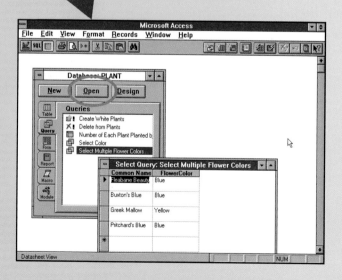

TASK 46

Selecting Records that Match Both Criteria

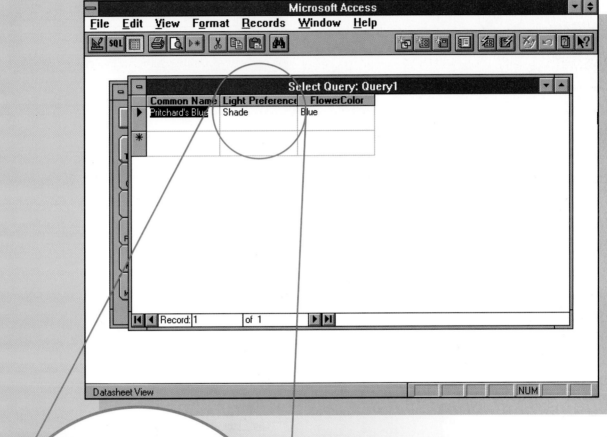

"Why would I do this?"

Often, you need to find records that meet multiple criteria—for example, all customers who live in California and made purchases in the past year. For a customer's record to be included in the answer dynaset, the record must meet both criteria. This is an example of using an *AND* operator.

In this task, you use the AND operator in a query that finds all plants that have blue flowers and prefer shade.

Task 46: Selecting Records that Match Both Criteria

1 From the Query list in the Database window, click the **New** button, and then click the **New Query** button in the New Query dialog box. In the Add Table dialog box, select the **Plants** table and click the **Add** button. The Plants field-name list appears at the top of the Select Query window. Click the **Close** button in the Add Table dialog box to remove it from view.

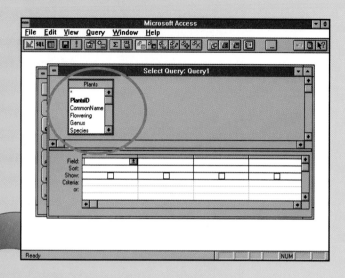

2 Select, by double-clicking, these fields in the Plants list: **CommonName**, **LightPreference**, and **FlowerColor**.

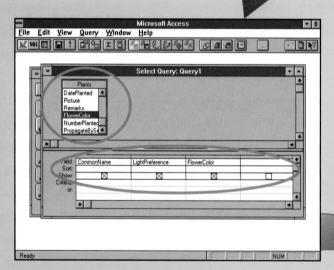

3 Type "**Shade**" in the Criteria row of the LightPreference column. Type "**Blue**" in the Criteria row of the FlowerColor column.

> **NOTE** ▼
>
> Whenever you want to select records that meet two criteria, place both criteria in the same row. If you want to select records that meet one criteria or another, place each criterion on a separate line.

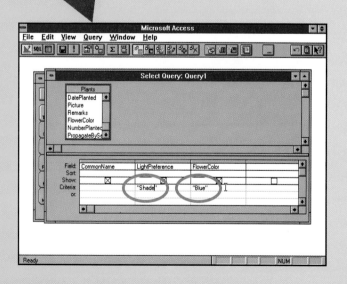

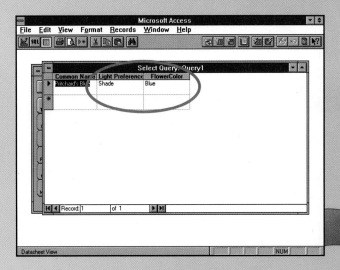

4 Click the **Run** button in the toolbar to display any records that meet your criteria.

5 Double-click the **Control menu** button in the Select Query window. Then click the **No** button to close the window without saving this query.

WHY WORRY?

If your answer dynaset includes records that do not meet both criteria that you entered, make sure that you entered both criteria in the same row. If you entered them in different rows, you may have told Access for Windows to use the OR operator, not the AND operator.

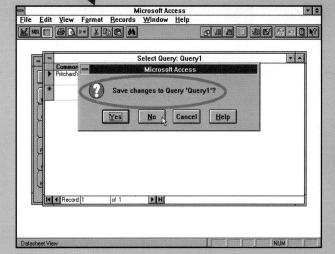

Using Arithmetic Operators

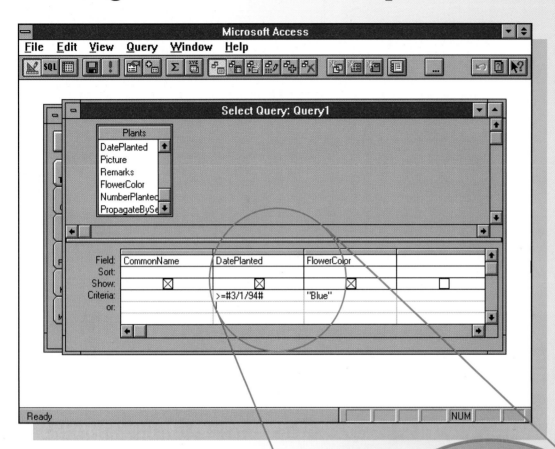

"Why would I do this?"

Arithmetic operators don't operate exclusively on number fields. You can use arithmetic operators to display all records for customers whose last names begin with the letter *F* to the letter *M*. The most commonly used arithmetic operators include = (equal), > (greater than), >= (greater than or equal to), < (less than), and <= (less than or equal to).

In this task, you create a select query that displays all plants that have blue flowers and were planted on or before March 1, 1994.

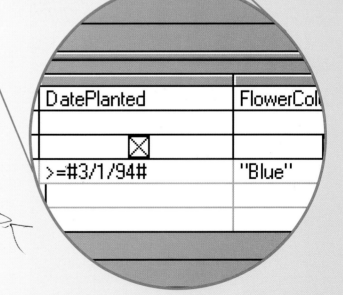

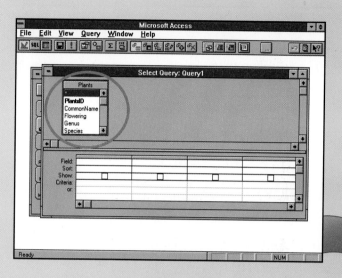

1 Open the New Query dialog box and click the **New Query** button. Select the **Plants** table for this query, and then close the Add Table dialog box.

2 In the Plants field-name list, select **CommonName**, **DatePlanted**, and **FlowerColor**.

> **NOTE** ▼
>
> Because this query requires the answers to meet both criteria, the query uses an AND operator. Enter both criteria in the same row.

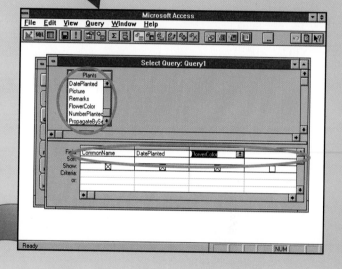

3 The first part of the query statement is *display all plants that have blue flowers.* Move the cursor to the Criteria row, and type **"Blue"**. Then move the cursor left one field to the DatePlanted column.

Task 47: Using Arithmetic Operators

4 Type **>=3/1/94** in the Criteria row of the DatePlanted column. Then click any other field. Notice that Access for Windows changes your entry to **>=#3/1/94#**, which indicates that this field is a number field. Remember that a date field can be used in a calculation and therefore is considered to be a number field.

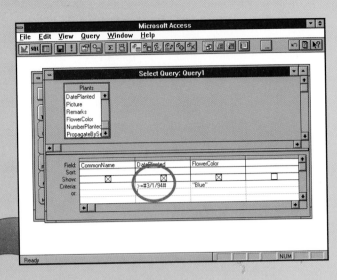

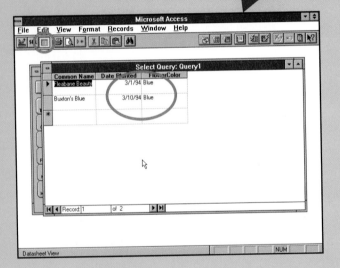

5 Click the **Run** button in the toolbar to view the answer dynaset for this query.

WHY WORRY?

If your query displays records that meet one or the other criterion, you made this an OR query by entering your criteria on separate lines. Make sure that your criteria statements are in the same line to create the AND query.

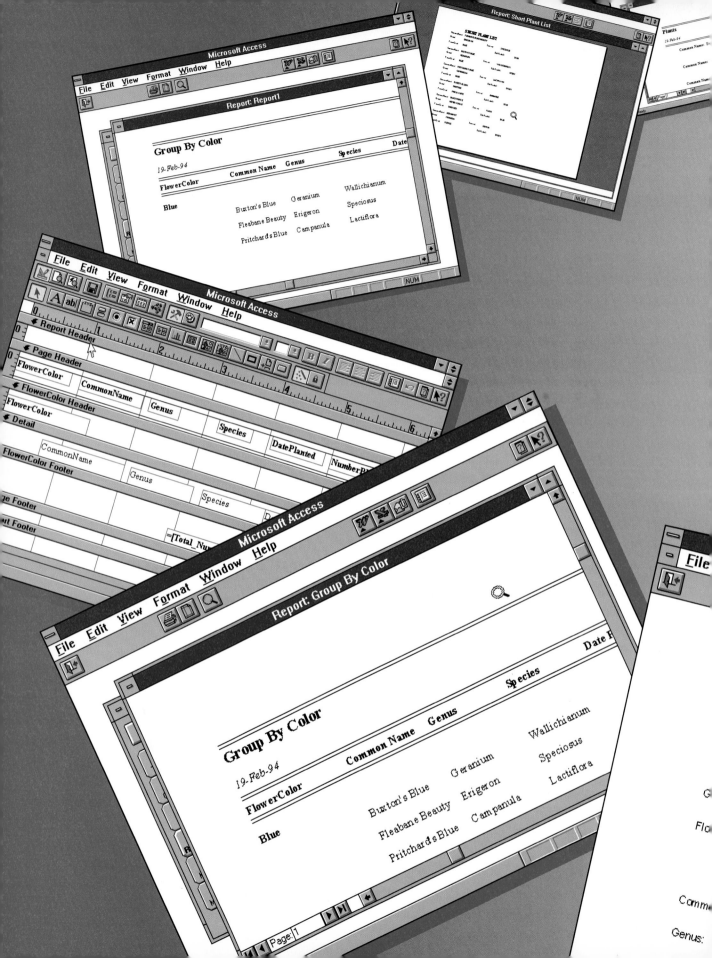

PART VI

Creating and Using Reports

Part VI: Creating and Using Reports

Until now, you have designed and used entry and selection tools that you will use on-screen. These skills alone are fine if you never have to show information to someone else or share information with a co-worker. Those situations seldom occur in the real world, however, so you also need to know how to create reports.

Although you can print copies of your tables, forms, and query results, you have greater control of the way information is presented in a report. In many ways, a report is similar to a form; you can choose how to group records within a report. You can create a report that displays subtotals for selected groups of records (or for each page) and a final total for the entire report.

Often, you will use a query to create an answer dynaset and then create a report based on that dynaset to present the information in an easy-to-understand format. By using a report, you can easily add summary information, such as totals, subtotals, and percentages.

You can create reports for a variety of purposes, including the following:

- Mailing labels

- Invoices

- Address and phone lists

- Analyses of sales and purchases

- Lists of sales contacts

- Account-collection letters

You can create a report by using a ReportWizard or by building your report from the Design View window. A report created with a ReportWizard is based on a single table. You can choose among seven ReportWizards:

Single-Column. With this Wizard, you can create a report that displays each field of each record in one column. A label appears to the left of each field.

Groups/Totals. Use this Wizard to create a report that displays information in tabular form. You can choose how you want your records to be grouped. A label appears at the top of each column. Group subtotals are included, and a final total appears at the end of the report.

Mailing Label. This Wizard helps you create professional mailing labels quickly. You can add text to each label, and select the order in which your labels are sorted. You also can use this Wizard to create shipping labels, product labels, and any other information that can be printed on standard sheet or continuous-feed labels.

Summary. With this Wizard, you can create a report similar to the Groups/Totals report, but without all the detailed information on each individual record. A summary report provides a subtotal for each group of records and a final total at the end of the report.

Tabular. This Wizard also creates a tabular report, displaying all fields for each record. Each record occupies one line. A label appears at the top of each column.

AutoReport. When you use this Wizard, Access for Windows automatically creates a report from the selected table. The report is in tabular format, with labels at the tops of columns.

Microsoft WordMail Merge. This Wizard helps you create a report and then merge it with a Microsoft Word document.

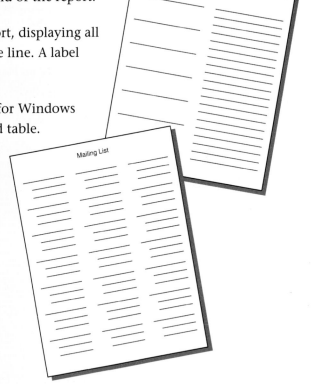

Creating a Report with a ReportWizard

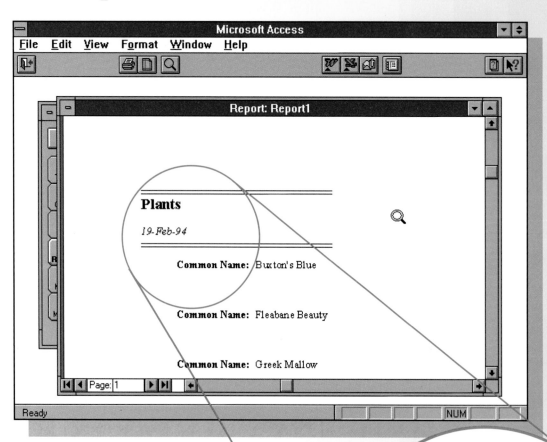

"Why would I do this?"

You have set up your table, created forms, and entered your information; you can use a query to extract information from your table. The boss wants a report on her desk by quitting time. By using a ReportWizard, you can quickly create a report with a polished, professional appearance. In this task, you use the Single-Column ReportWizard to create a report.

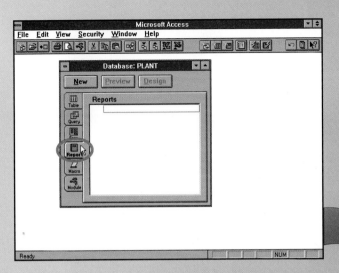

1 Open the Database window and click the **Report** button. You see the Reports list box. Because you have not yet created any reports, the list is blank.

2 Click the **New** button. You see the New Report dialog box. Select the table or query on which you want to base the report; click the **down-arrow** button beside the text box to display a drop-down list of available tables and queries.

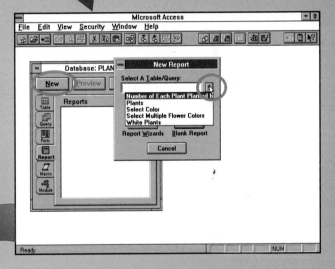

3 Choose the table Plants from the list, and then click the **ReportWizards** button. Now select the first option in the list box **Single-Column**, which is the ReportWizard you want to use.

4 Click **OK** to move to the next dialog box in which you select the fields you want to include in the report. Click the **>>** button to select all fields.

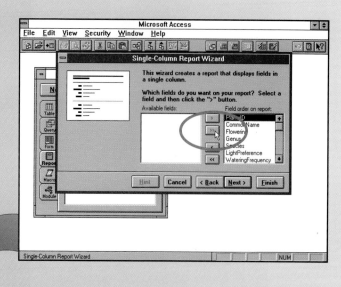

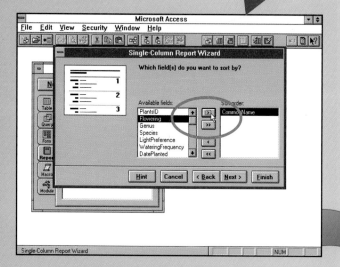

5 Click the **Next >** button to move to the next dialog box. Select the field **CommonName**, on which you will sort your report, and then click the **>** button.

6 Click the **Next >** button again to move to the next dialog box. The default settings in this dialog box work well for most reports, but you can experiment with other styles.

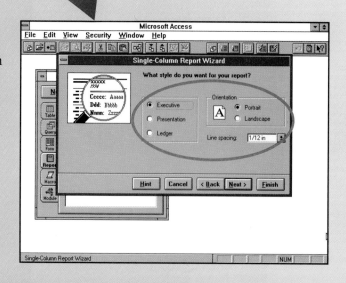

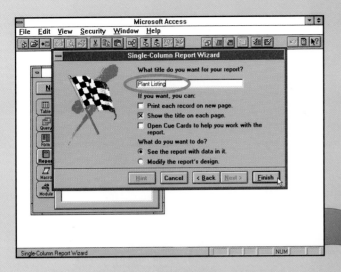

7 Click the **Next >** button. Type **Plant Listing** in the text box as the title of this report.

8 Click the **Finish** button again. You see the report displayed in a window in the actual size at which it will print. Notice that the mouse pointer changes shape in the report window, becoming a magnifying glass.

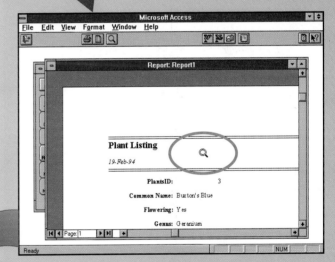

WHY WORRY?

You always can re-create a report that you created with a ReportWizard. Unless you make formatting changes in a ReportWizard report, you do not need to save it.

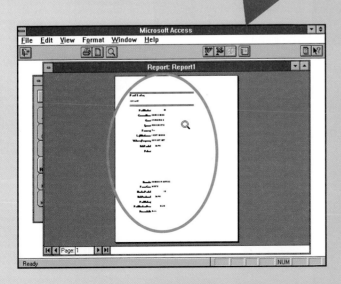

9 Click the left mouse button while the mouse pointer is in the Report window. You see the entire first page of the report. Although you cannot read the report, this method is a good way to see how a page is formatted. To close the window without saving this report, press **Ctrl+F4** and then click the **No** button.

Creating a Report in Design View

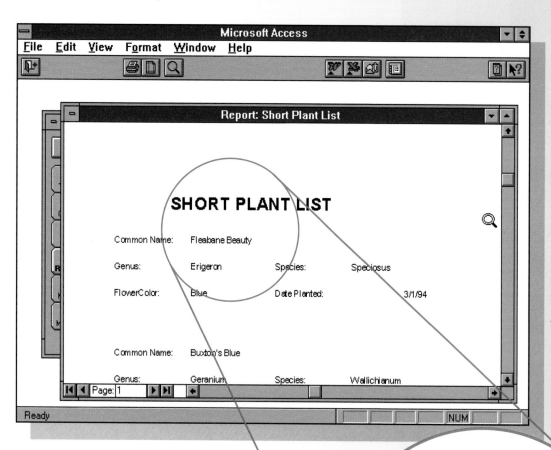

"Why would I do this?"

Any time you want to customize a report created with a ReportWizard or to create a unique report, you do so in the Design View window. Creating a report in Design view is almost identical to creating a form in Design view.

In this task, you use Design view to create a simple report.

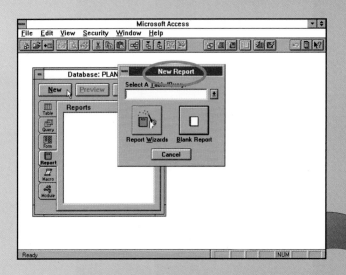

1 Open the Database window, and click the **Report** button. Then click the **New** button. The New Report dialog box appears.

2 Click the **down-arrow** button, and select the table Plants from the list. Then click the **Blank Report** button. The Design View Report window appears.

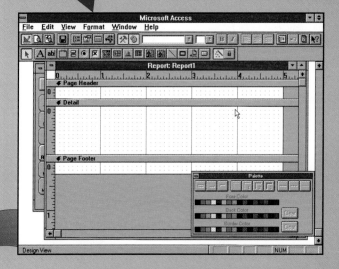

3 Click the **Field List** button in the top toolbar. You see the Plants list, displaying the fields available for your report.

Task 49: Creating a Report in Design View

4 Click and drag the **CommonName** field from the field name list to the detail area of the report.

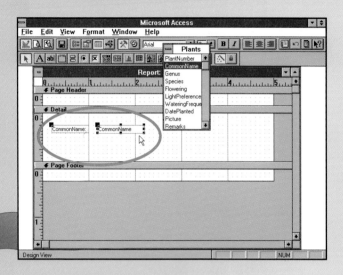

5 Drag and drop the fields **Genus**, **Species**, **FlowerColor**, and **DatePlanted** into the detail area of your report. Close the Field list window by double-clicking the **Control menu** button.

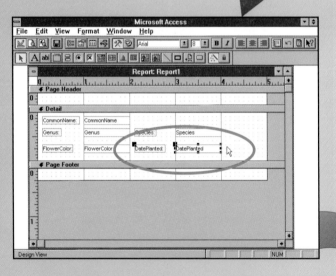

NOTE ▼

Remember that you can drag the Page Footer bar down to increase the size of the report detail area if you want to use more fields than will fit in the default area.

6 Click the **Label** button in the second toolbar, and move the mouse pointer to the Page Header area. Drag a label box into the header area. Type **Short Plant List** and press **Enter** to select the label box.

NOTE ▼

To change the text that you entered, you must select the label box. Access for Windows then acts on all the text within the box.

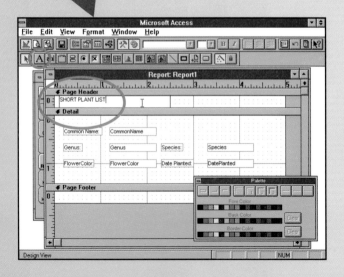

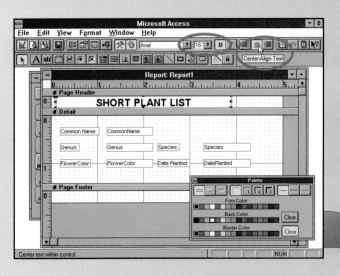

7 Click the Font Size **down-arrow** button in the first toolbar. Select a font size of **16** points for this text. Click the **Font Bold** button, and then click the **Center Alignment** button to center the label in the label box.

8 Click the **Save** button in the first toolbar. Type **Short Plant List** in the text box as the name for this report, and then click the **OK** button.

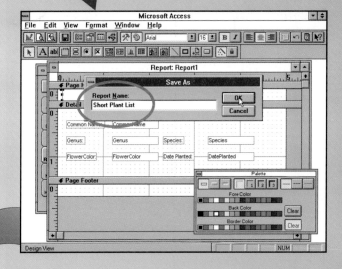

9 Click the **Sample Preview** button in the first toolbar. You see what your report will look like when it prints. Click the **Close Window** button to return to Design view, where you can make any necessary changes. Press **Ctrl+F4** to close the Report Design View window.

Creating a Grouped Report with Totals

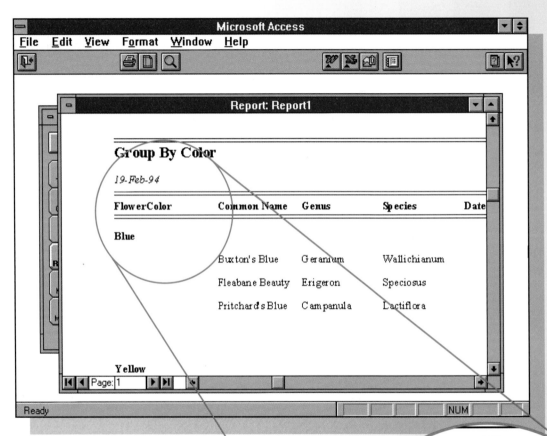

"Why would I do this?"

You will find that your information is easier to understand when similar items or records are grouped rather than listed separately, as they are in your table. You also can display subtotals for each group, such as number of records, numbers of items, or value of items. In this task, you create a report grouped by flower color, with totals for the number of plants now planted.

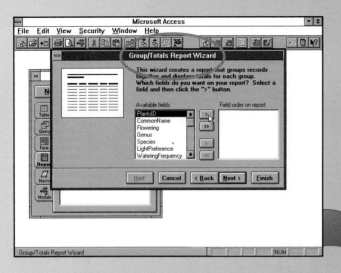

1 Open the Database window, click the **Report** button, click the **New** button, and then click the **down-arrow** button and select the table Plants from the list. Click the **ReportWizards** button. Select the **Groups/Totals** Wizard from the ReportWizard dialog box, and click the **OK** button. The Groups/Totals ReportWizard dialog box appears.

2 Select the following fields, clicking the > button after each selection to add that field to the field order on report list: **CommonName**, **Genus**, **Species**, **DatePlanted**, **FlowerColor**, and **NumberPlanted**.

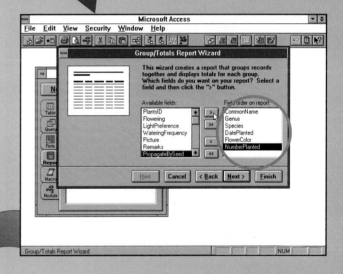

3 Click the **Next >** button to move to the next dialog box. Select **FlowerColor** as the field on which you want to group your records.

4 Click the **Next >** button to open the next dialog box. In the Group box, select **Normal**. This option will group all records that contain the same flower color.

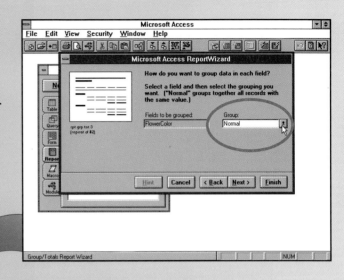

5 Click the **Next >** button to open the next dialog box. Select **CommonName** as the field on which to sort your records.

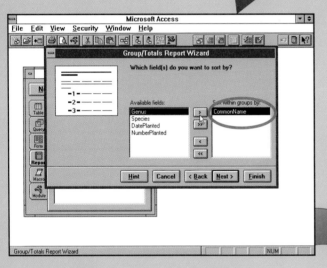

6 Click the **Next >** button again. Because this report type creates a tabular report, with fields displayed across the page, use the default page-orientation option (Landscape). This option enables you to show the maximum amount of information on each page.

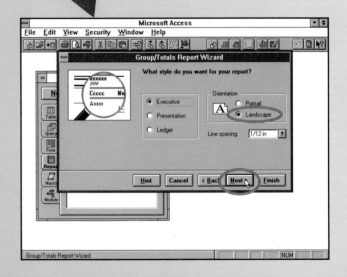

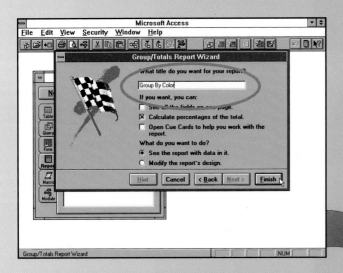

7 Click the **Next >** button to see the next dialog box. Type **Group By Color** in the text box as the title for this report.

8 Click the **Finish** button. You see your report on-screen, with your plant records grouped according to flower color. Press **Ctrl+F4** to close the window.

> **NOTE** ▼
>
> Clicking the Close Window button in the toolbar displays a new report in the Report Design View window. You then can make any necessary adjustments to the report's design. After you save your report, click the Close Window button to return to the Database window.

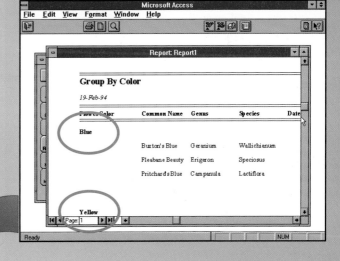

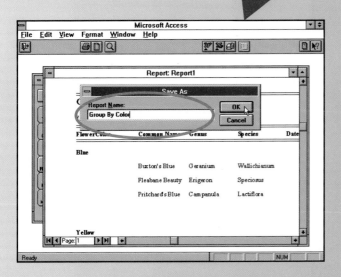

9 Click the **Yes** button in the Save Changes dialog box, and then type **Group By Color** in the Save As dialog box. Click the **OK** button to save your report. You now see the report listed in the Report list of the Database window.

TASK 51
Adding and Deleting Headers and Footers

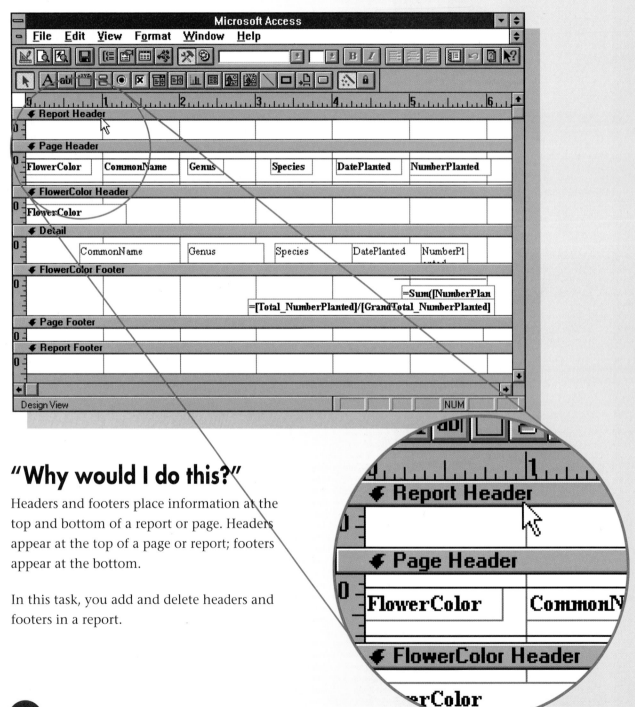

"Why would I do this?"

Headers and footers place information at the top and bottom of a report or page. Headers appear at the top of a page or report; footers appear at the bottom.

In this task, you add and delete headers and footers in a report.

Task 51: Adding and Deleting Headers and Footers

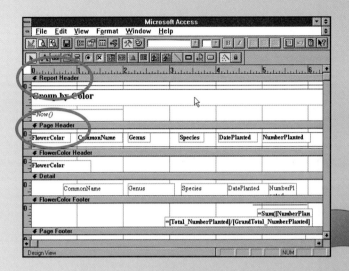

1 Open the Report list in the Database window. Select the **Group By Color** report, and click the **Design** button. The report appears in the Report Design View window. As you can see, this report includes headers and footers for the report and for each page.

NOTE ▼

Headers and footers are created or deleted in pairs. If you add a page header, you also have to add a page footer.

2 Delete the report header and footer by clicking the **Format** menu, and then clicking the **Report Header/Footer** option in the drop-down menu. Click the **OK** button in the confirmation dialog box to remove the report header and footer.

NOTE ▼

When you delete a header, you also delete its paired footer. You cannot use the Undo command to restore a deleted header and footer.

3 Add the report header and footer back into your report by selecting **Format** in the menu bar and then choosing **Report Header/Footer** from the drop-down menu. Access places a blank report header band and blank report footer band in your report. You can quickly size the bands to accommodate the necessary information and then add labels and summary fields as needed.

Opening or Previewing a Report

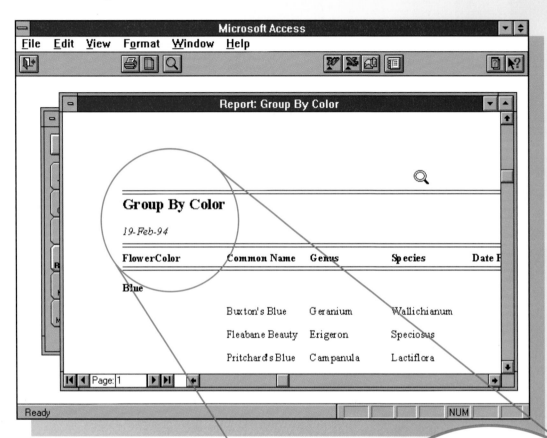

"Why would I do this?"

When you want to use a report, either by displaying it or by making a hard copy with your printer, you first must open the report. When you open a report, it appears in a report window, which enables you to view the report before you print it.

In this task, you open and display a report.

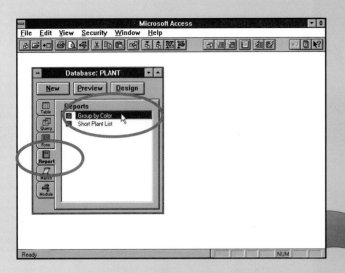

1 Open the Database window. Click the **Report** button and then select the report Group by Color. Click the **Preview** button to view your report.

2 You see your report.

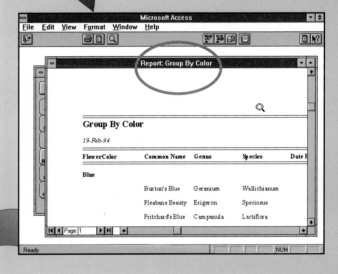

3 Click the **Close Window** button to return to the Database window.

WHY WORRY?

If your report does not contain the information you want or is too detailed, you can edit the report in the Report Design View window or use a query to extract more specific information.

Printing a Report

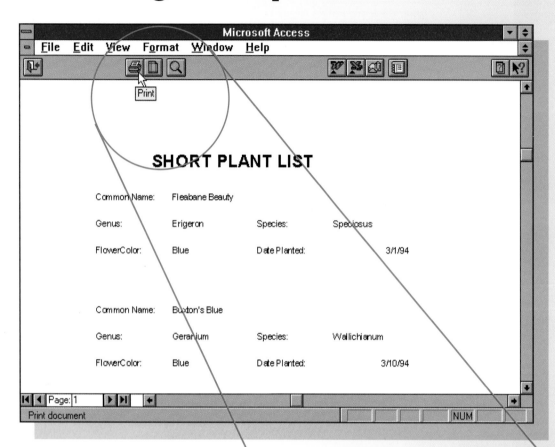

"Why would I do this?"

You have designed, changed, and viewed the reports that you created, and they look great on-screen. Now you are ready to show a larger audience how well you have done, and for that purpose, you must print a copy of your report. You can print a report from either the Database window or the report preview window.

In this task, you print a report.

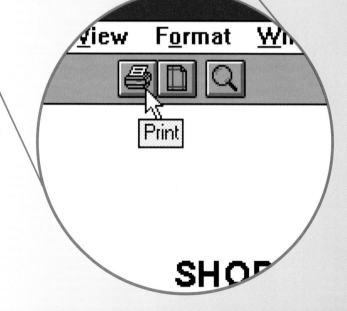

1 Open the Database window, click the **Report** button, and select the report **Group by Color**. Then click the **Print** button in the toolbar. The Print dialog box appears.

NOTE ▼

You can also select File from the menu, and then choose Print from the drop-down menu.

2 Click the **OK** button in the Print dialog box to begin printing the report. When Access for Windows sends the report to your printer, you return to the Database window.

NOTE ▼

You also can print a report from the report preview window by clicking the Print button in the toolbar.

WHY WORRY?

If your printer jams, you can use the Print dialog box to resume printing your report from a specified page.

PART VII

Managing Database Files

Part VII: Managing Database Files

Up to now, you have been concerned primarily with information that you entered into Access for Windows. You have entered information into a table and into a form, extracted information with a query, and displayed and printed information as a report. As you worked with your information, you were working within a single database file and four database objects: the table, the form, the query, and the report.

As you continue to work with your database, you will find that entering information and occasionally creating a new table or form are not the only tasks involved in managing a database. You also may need to do the following:

- Copy tables or forms so that a co-worker can use your information.

- Make a backup copy of your database.

- Create copies of information, giving each copy a different name.

- Rename a table.

- Delete obsolete tables, forms, and other objects from your computer's hard disk.

In addition, the information contained in your database is valuable and may require protection. Some records, such as personnel and payroll records, can contain sensitive information to which other employees should not have access. Access for Windows enables you to assign passwords to your information. If you share your database with other people and want to protect sensitive information, or if you do not want someone to be able to change or add information, a password will help protect your records.

The Security option in your Access for Windows menu enables you to assign different passwords to different users of your database. Each person who uses your information should have a unique password. You also can assign permissions for each user, or group of users. *Permissions* restrict the activities that other people can perform. For example, you can give your sales staff permissions to view customer sales histories and inventory information, but not allow them to alter the information. By using passwords and permissions, you can create an environment that both fosters the use of information and provides adequate security for that information.

Copying Database Files

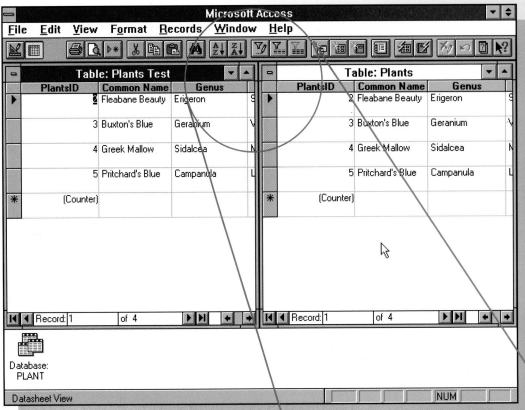

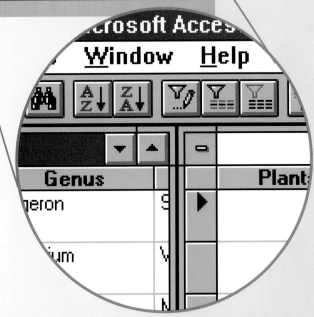

"Why would I do this?"

When you need to share your information with a co-worker, create a backup of a table or duplicate a table or form so you can experiment with it; simply make a copy. You can explore various changes in the object, table, form, query, or report until it fits your needs. Working with a copy of your database object enables you to retain the original safely.

In this task, you copy a table. You can use the same technique to copy any other database object.

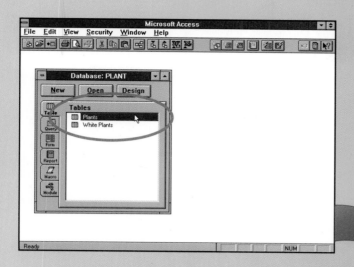

1 Open the Database window, and click the **Table** button. Select the table **Plants** from the Tables list.

> **NOTE** ▼
>
> Select other database objects to be copied by clicking the appropriate button in the Database window and then selecting the specific form (or other object) from the list.

2 Click the **Copy** button in the toolbar. Access for Windows copies the table to the Windows Clipboard.

3 Now click the **Paste** button.

Task 54: Copying Database Files

4 In the Paste Table As dialog box, type **Plants Test** as the name for this copy of your table. You cannot use the same name as your original. Click the **OK** button.

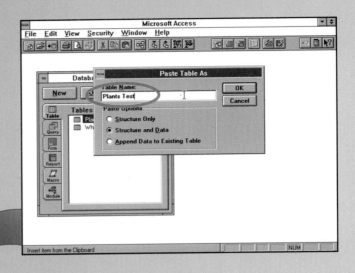

NOTE ▼

By default, Access for Windows copies both the structure and data for the new table. You can direct the program to copy only the table structure, creating a table with identical fields but no information in those fields. You also can add the copied records to another table.

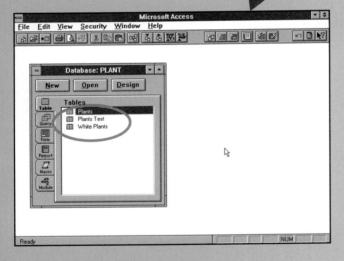

5 You see the newly copied table in the Tables list.

WHY WORRY?

If you do not need your copied table or form later, simply delete it from the list.

Renaming a
Database Table

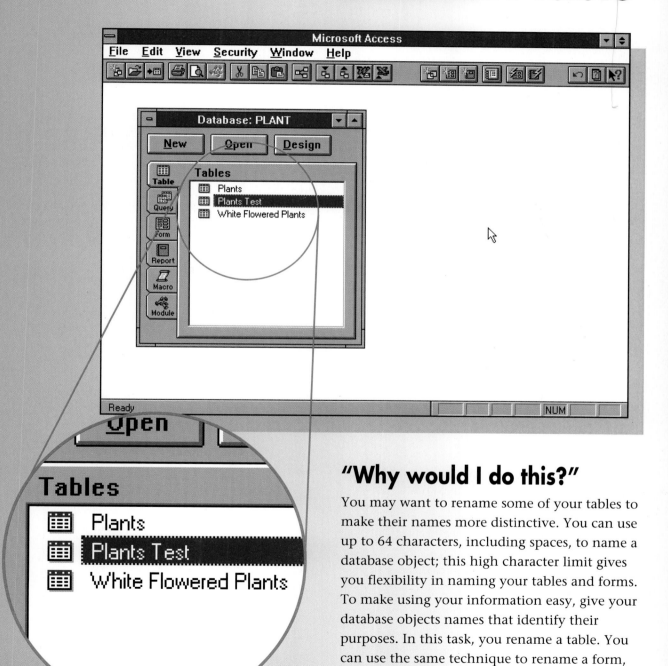

"Why would I do this?"

You may want to rename some of your tables to make their names more distinctive. You can use up to 64 characters, including spaces, to name a database object; this high character limit gives you flexibility in naming your tables and forms. To make using your information easy, give your database objects names that identify their purposes. In this task, you rename a table. You can use the same technique to rename a form, query, or report.

Task 55: Renaming a Database Table

1 Select the table name **White Plants** from the list. Then choose **File** from the menu bar, and choose **Rename** from the drop-down menu.

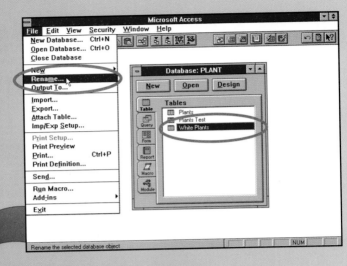

2 In the Rename dialog box, type **White Flowered Plants**. Click the **OK** button.

3 You see the table listed with its new name.

WHY WORRY?

If you find that you misspelled the name of your table, simply rename the table.

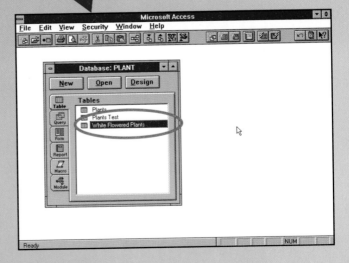

Deleting Database Files

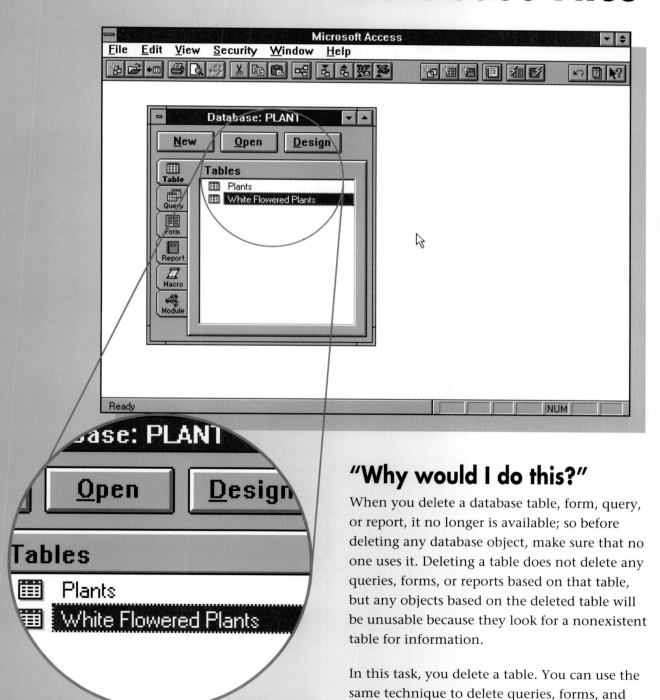

"Why would I do this?"

When you delete a database table, form, query, or report, it no longer is available; so before deleting any database object, make sure that no one uses it. Deleting a table does not delete any queries, forms, or reports based on that table, but any objects based on the deleted table will be unusable because they look for a nonexistent table for information.

In this task, you delete a table. You can use the same technique to delete queries, forms, and reports.

Task 56: Deleting Database Files

1 From the Database window's Table list, select the new table **Plants Test**.

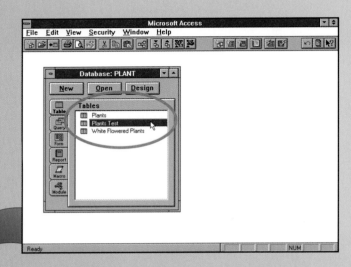

2 Choose **Edit** from the menu bar, and then choose **Delete** from the drop-down menu.

3 Click the **OK** button in the dialog box. Access for Windows removes the table named Plants Test from the Tables list.

WHY WORRY?

If you deleted the wrong table or decide that you really don't want to delete that form, you can click the Undo button (or choose Undo from the Edit menu) to restore the deleted database object.

Adding Password Protection

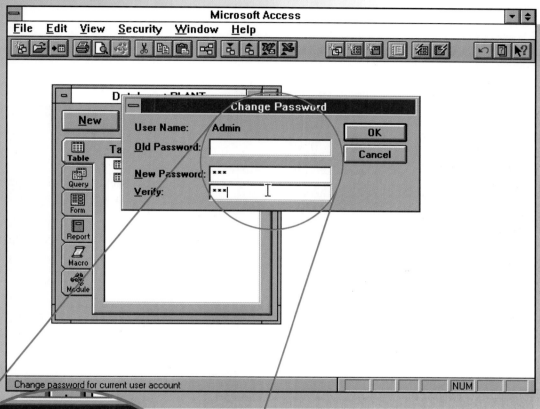

"Why would I do this?"

A password restricts access to your database by allowing only people who have the correct password to open Access for Windows. Any database that contains company information has value to that company. Personnel and payroll records contain sensitive information that should not be available to any casual user.

In this task, you add a password to your copy of Access for Windows.

Task 57: Adding Password Protection

1 With the Database window open, choose the **Security** menu, and then choose the **Change Password** option. The Change Password dialog box appears.

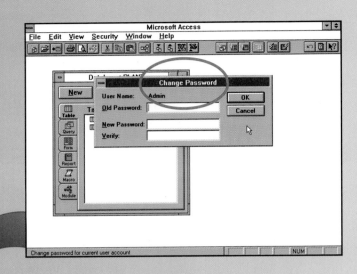

NOTE ▼

When you add a password to Access, you will be assigned a login name, Admin, that has all allowable rights to the database. When you log in to Access with a password, you will also be asked for your login name. When you want to change an existing password, enter it in the Old Password text box.

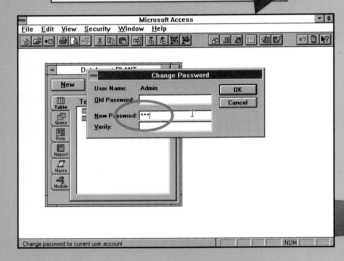

2 Click the New Password text box to select it, and type **ABC** as your new password. Notice that only asterisks appear in the text box as you type. No matter what you enter as a password, asterisks are all you will ever see when you enter your password.

NOTE ▼

Passwords always are case-sensitive. When you create (and use) a password, make sure that you correctly use uppercase and lowercase letters.

3 Press the **Tab** key to move the cursor to the Verify text box, and type your password again. Then click the **OK** button. Access for Windows accepts and assigns your password.

NOTE ▼

If you do not repeat in the Verify text box the exact password that you entered in the New Password text box, Access displays a dialog box telling you that you did not match the password.

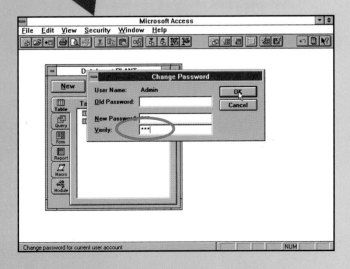

Deleting a Password

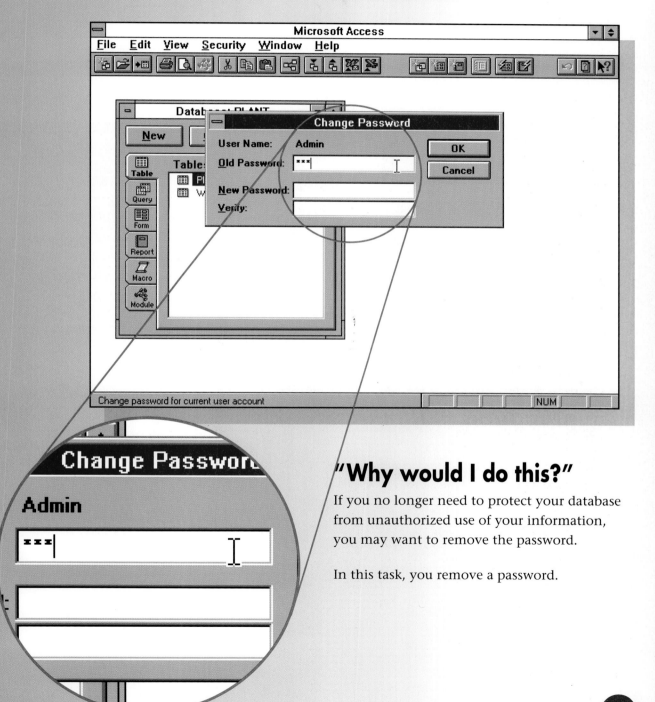

"Why would I do this?"

If you no longer need to protect your database from unauthorized use of your information, you may want to remove the password.

In this task, you remove a password.

Task 58: Deleting a Password

1 Choose **Security** from the menu bar, and then choose the **Change Password** option. The Change Password dialog box appears.

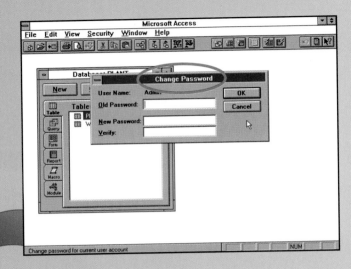

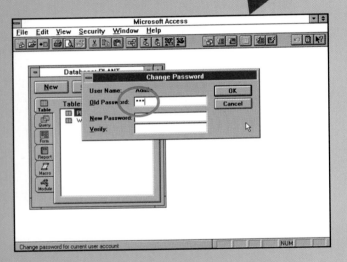

2 Type your current, or old, password **ABC** in the Old Password text box, and then click the **OK** button. Because you did not enter anything in the New Password and Verify text boxes, Access for Windows understands that no password was assigned.

WHY WORRY?

You always can add a password back to your database if you feel that the additional protection is needed.

Adding Permissions

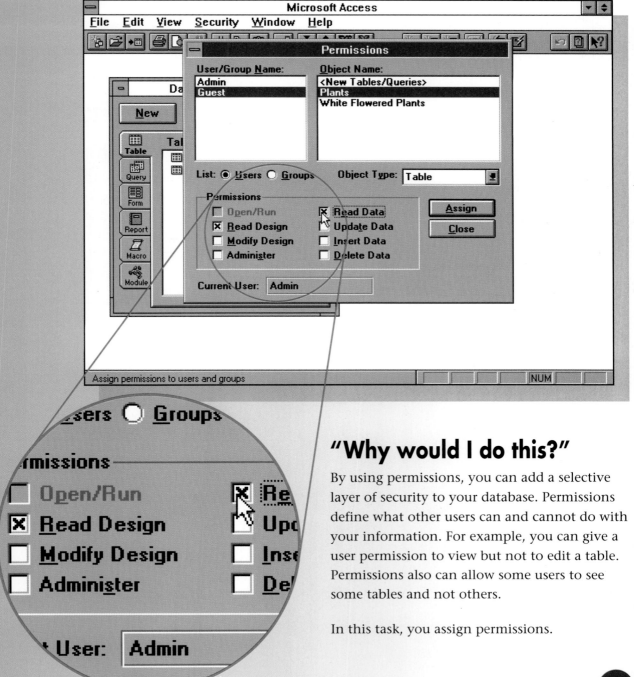

"Why would I do this?"

By using permissions, you can add a selective layer of security to your database. Permissions define what other users can and cannot do with your information. For example, you can give a user permission to view but not to edit a table. Permissions also can allow some users to see some tables and not others.

In this task, you assign permissions.

Task 59: Adding Permissions

1 Choose **Security** from the menu bar, and then choose **Permissions** from the drop-down menu. The Permissions dialog box appears.

WHY WORRY?

Permissions that you assign do not become effective until you exit Access for Windows and then open it again.

2 Select the **Guest** option in the User/Group Name list box so you can assign permissions for a guest or temporary user of your database. Then select the table **Plants** from the Object Name list box.

NOTE ▼

The Admin user always has the highest level of access to the database. You never should place restricted permissions on this user or group name.

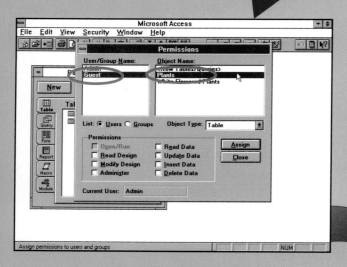

3 Click the option **Read Data**. The Read Design option is automatically selected along with Read Data. Access assumes that if a user is allowed to read table information, that user also can read the design of the table. Click the **Assign** button to assign the guest user permission to view the information in the Plants table.

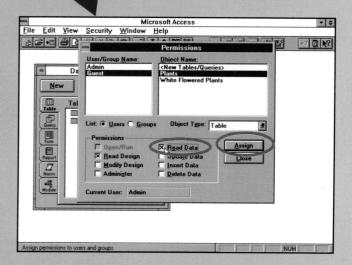

Using a Password-Protected Database

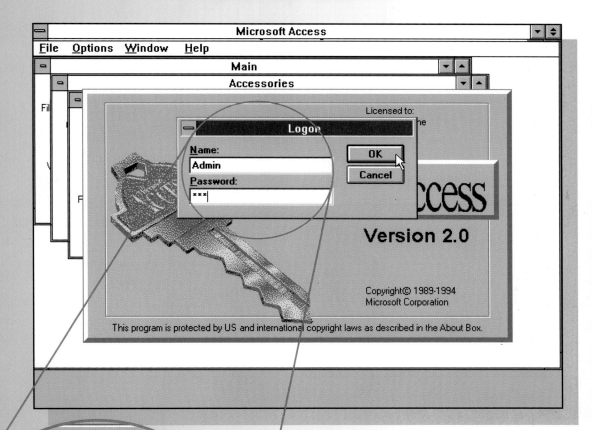

"Why would I do this?"

After you assign passwords and permissions to your database, you must use your password to open Access for Windows. When you open the program with password protection, you must enter your password in a dialog box before Access for Windows finishes loading itself into your computer's memory.

In this task, you open Access for Windows with a password.

Task 60: Using a Password-Protected Database

1 From the Windows Program Manager, choose the **Microsoft Access** icon.

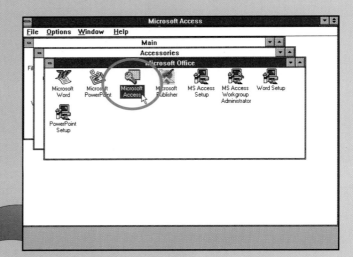

2 Enter your user name in the Name text box, and then type your password in the Password text box of the Logon dialog box. Click the **OK** button.

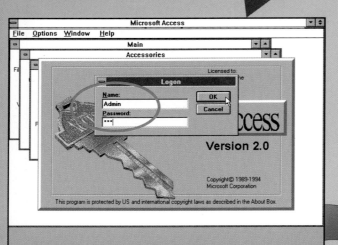

NOTE ▼

If you do not enter a correct user name or password, Access for Windows displays a dialog box telling you so. Click the OK button in this dialog box and try again.

3 Access for Windows opens on-screen.

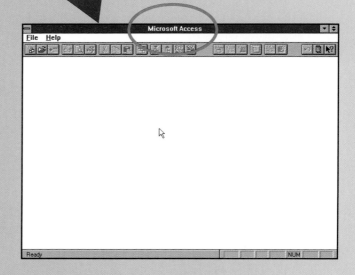

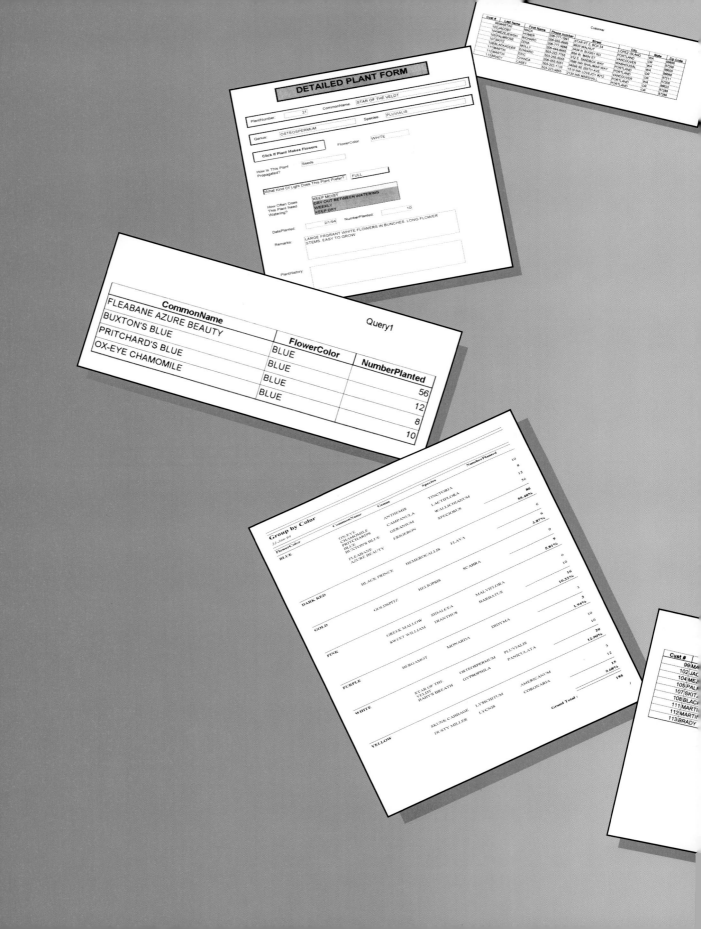

Sample Documents

▼ Create a table document

▼ Create a data entry form

▼ Create a query answer document

▼ Create a report document

Part VIII: Sample Documents

Date of Report, page 32

Table Name, page 22

Field Labels, page 32

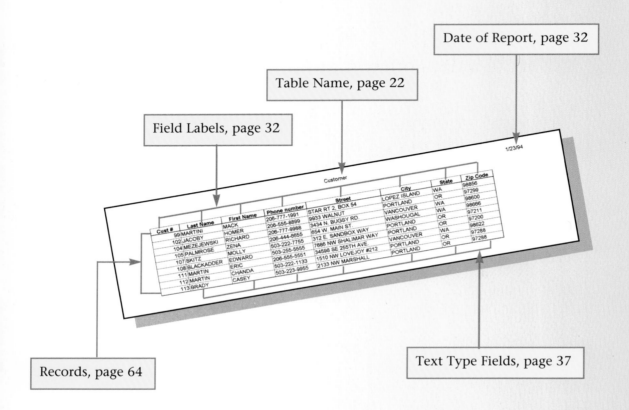

Records, page 64

Text Type Fields, page 37

Create a Table Document

Building a table was discussed in Part II of this book. To create a table you must follow these procedures:

1 Create the table by clicking the Table button on the Database window and then selecting the New button. To create a table from scratch using the Table Design View window, click the New Table button. You can also create a table using Table Wizards. See this task for help:

Creating a New Database Table   *page 32*

2 Add fields to your table by typing a field name and then selecting a field type. See this task for help:

Entering a New Field   *page 37*

3 Number type fields are used for fields that will contain only numeric information, such as quantities and prices. See this task for help:

Creating Number Type Fields   *page 40*

4 Add counter fields by typing the field name and then selecting Counter as the field type. Use counter fields when you need to provide a unique identifying number to each record. Examples of this would include customer numbers or invoice numbers.

5 Delete a field from your table by highlighting the field description in the Table Design View window and pressing the Delete key. See this task for help:

Deleting a Field   *page 57*

Part VIII: Sample Documents

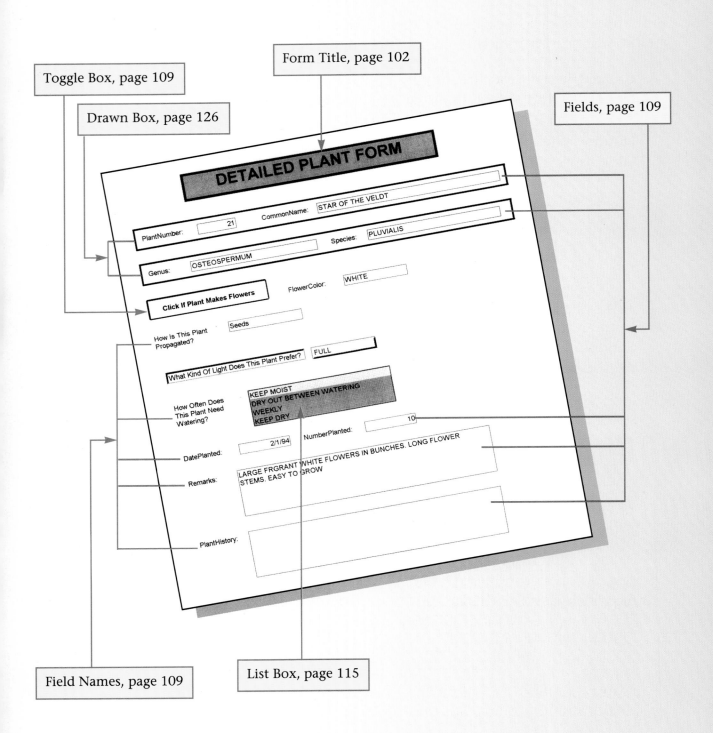

Toggle Box, page 109

Drawn Box, page 126

Form Title, page 102

Fields, page 109

DETAILED PLANT FORM

PlantNumber: 21   CommonName: STAR OF THE VELDT

Species: PLUVIALIS

Genus: OSTEOSPERMUM

Click If Plant Makes Flowers   FlowerColor: WHITE

How Is This Plant Propagated? Seeds

What Kind Of Light Does This Plant Prefer? FULL

KEEP MOIST
DRY OUT BETWEEN WATERING
WEEKLY
KEEP DRY

How Often Does This Plant Need Watering?

NumberPlanted: 10

DatePlanted: 2/1/94

Remarks: LARGE FRGRANT WHITE FLOWERS IN BUNCHES. LONG FLOWER STEMS. EASY TO GROW

PlantHistory:

Field Names, page 109

List Box, page 115

Create a Data Entry Form

In Part IV of this book, you learn how to create and use a form. The basic steps to create a form include:

1 Use the Form Wizards to design a completed form, or open the Form Design window to create your form from scratch. See the following task for help:

2 Add fields to your form by clicking the Field List button and then dragging selected fields to the location on the form where you want them placed. See this task for help:

3 Use text labels on your form as titles and to include blocks of instructions if needed. See this task for help:

4 Use a list box to restrict the entry into a field to one answer from a list of specified answers. See this task:

5 Use a combo box to select a single answer from a drop-down list of answers for a field or to type your own answer. See this task for help:

6 Toggle buttons can be used when an answer is limited to Yes/No or True/False. See this task for help:

7 Draw boxes and lines as necessary to help differentiate portions of your form. See this task:

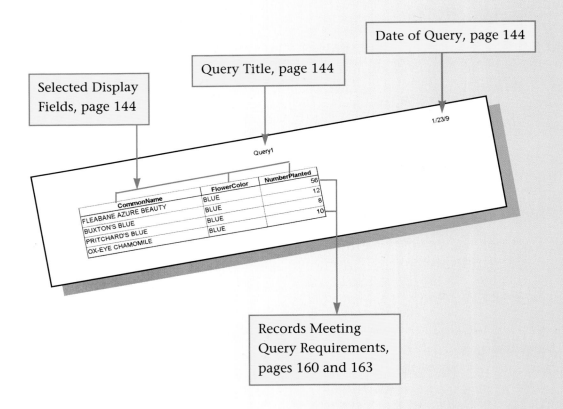

Selected Display Fields, page 144

Query Title, page 144

Date of Query, page 144

Records Meeting Query Requirements, pages 160 and 163

Create a Query Answer Document

In Part V of this book, you learn to ask questions and extract information from your database by using a query statement:

1 Select specific records using a Select Query. See this task for help:

> *Creating a Select Query*   *page 144*

2 Summarize information contained in your table using a Crosstab Query. See this task for help:

> *Using a Crosstab Query*   *page 149*

3 Use an Action Query to delete, add, or archive selected records from a table or from one table to another. See this task for help:

> *Creating an Action Query*   *page 153*

4 If you are not sure of the spelling of a record to be selected, or if you want to include all records that have a similar spelling, use wild-card characters in your query statement. See this task for help:

> *Choosing Records Using Wild Cards*   *page 157*

5 When you want to see records that meet one or another criteria, use the OR operator when creating the query statement. See this task for help:

> *Selecting Records that Match Criteria*   *page 160*

6 To select records that must meet more than one criteria in order to be selected, use an AND operator. See this task for help:

> *Selecting Records that Match Both Criteria*   *page 163*

Part VIII: Sample Documents

Report Title, page 186

Report Date, page 186

Report Field Names, page 174

Report Records, page 174

Subtotal by Group, page 182

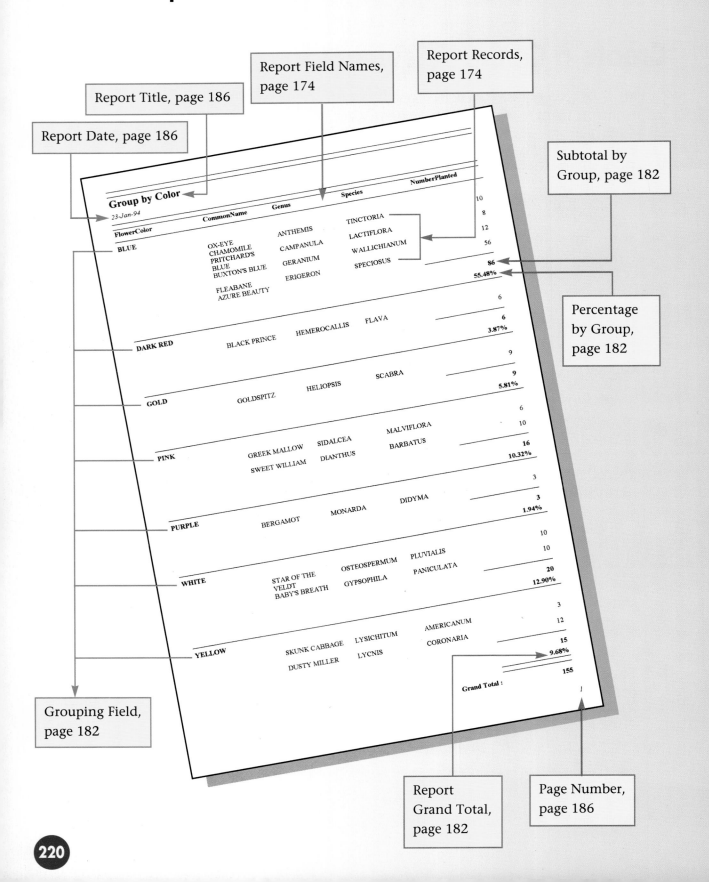

Group by Color				NumberPlanted
	CommonName	Genus	Species	
23-Jan-94				10
			TINCTORIA	8
FlowerColor			LACTIFLORA	12
BLUE	OX-EYE	ANTHEMIS	WALLICHIANUM	56
	CHAMOMILE	CAMPANULA		
	PRITCHARD'S	GERANIUM	SPECIOSUS	86
	BLUE			55.48%
	BUXTON'S BLUE	ERIGERON		
	FLEABANE			
	AZURE BEAUTY			
				6
		HEMEROCALLIS	FLAVA	6
DARK RED	BLACK PRINCE			3.87%
				9
		HELIOPSIS	SCABRA	9
GOLD	GOLDSPITZ			5.81%
			MALVIFLORA	6
	GREEK MALLOW	SIDALCEA	BARBATUS	10
PINK	SWEET WILLIAM	DIANTHUS		16
				10.32%
			DIDYMA	3
PURPLE	BERGAMOT	MONARDA		3
				1.94%
			PLUVIALIS	10
	STAR OF THE	OSTEOSPERMUM	PANICULATA	10
WHITE	VELDT	GYPSOPHILA		20
	BABY'S BREATH			12.90%
			AMERICANUM	3
	SKUNK CABBAGE	LYSICHITUM	CORONARIA	12
YELLOW	DUSTY MILLER	LYCNIS		15
				9.68%
				155
Grand Total :				1

Percentage by Group, page 182

Grouping Field, page 182

Report Grand Total, page 182

Page Number, page 186

Create a Report Document

In Part VI, you learn how to create and use the Report Design View window:

1 Create a report by selecting the Report button in the Database window and then clicking the New button. See this task for help:

> *Creating a Report in Design View*   *page 178*

2 Grouping records by a selected field makes a report more readable. See this task for help:

> *Creating a Grouped Report with Totals*   *page 182*

3 From the Report Design View window you can add or delete report or page headers and footers. See this task for help:

> *Adding and Deleting Headers and Footers*   *page 186*

PART IX
Glossary

Glossary

Action Query   A query that performs a specific action, such as moving, deleting, or copying selected records.

Active   The window or other database object that you are currently working in.

Alignment Buttons   Toolbar buttons that help you align data in a table field, a report, or a form.

AND Operator   Used to require two or more criteria be met for records to be selected in a query.

Append Query   A query that adds selected records from one table to another table.

Archive Query   A query that copies selected records from one table to another table, and then deletes these records from the first table.

Buttons   A picture representation of an action. Pressing a button (placing the mouse pointer on the button and then clicking the left mouse button) performs a selected command.

Check Box   A box that you click in to select an option.

Clipboard   A temporary memory area used by Windows programs, such as Microsoft Access, to cut or copy information to and paste information from.

Column Headings   The name, or label, given to a fixed column of information in a table, report, query, or form.

Combo Box   A selection box used in a form. You can either select an option from the displayed list, or enter your own value in the text box.

Copy   The Copy command, from either the Copy button or the Edit menu, will copy the information that you have selected and place it on the Windows Clipboard. The original information is not affected.

Counter Field   A numeric field that Microsoft Access uses to generate an automatic numbering system as you add records to a table. You cannot change the value of a counter field.

Criteria   A set of restrictions that you place on a query so that only records that meet your specifications will be selected.

Crosstab Query   A query used to present selected information in a spreadsheet format. This query type is most often used to present summary information about records in terms of a field, such as sales by region.

Currency Field   A type of number field that displays only currency values.

Cut   The command from either the toolbar or the Edit menu that deletes selected information from a table or form. The cut information is placed on the Windows Clipboard.

Data   Information in the form of text and numeric values entered into a table or form.

Database   A file of information about a related topic or purpose. Each database can contain one or more tables, forms, queries, reports, and other database objects.

Datasheet View   A window displaying in a row and column format.

Date Field   A field that contains date values.

Default   An action or selection that is automatically chosen by Access for Windows unless you specify another setting.

Delete Query   A query that deletes selected records from a table.

Design View   A window that displays the design of a table, form, query, or report. You can edit the existing database object in the Design View window, or create a new object.

Drag   A method used to select information with a mouse. Press and hold the left mouse button, and then drag the mouse pointer across the information to be selected. Release the mouse button when you reach the end of the information to be selected.

Dynaset   The set of selected records that results from running a query.

Field List   A list box of all fields from the selected table that is displayed in the Form, Report, and Query Design View window.

Fields   The smallest category of information contained in a record. Each column of a table contains a single field of information, such as Last Name, Customer Number, or ZIP Code.

Find   A command available through the Edit menu or toolbar that enables you to search for selected information in the active table.

Font   The style, size, and typeface of your characters.

Footers   Text that is displayed at the bottom of a group, page, or report. Footers can be used in forms and reports, and are often used to provide summary information.

Form   A view of information contained in your database. Usually a complete, single record is displayed in each form.

Glossary

Grid   A series of dotted lines and columns used in both the Form and Report Design View windows to help you place fields, labels, and other controls.

Headers   Text displayed at the top of a group, page, or report. Headers are often used to display labels and other information that you want to repeat.

Label   A block of text used as a caption, or instructions for a form, or a caption for a report.

List Box   A control used in a form that allows you to select an option from among a specified group of options.

Menu Bar   The horizontal bar directly below the title bar that contains the menu options.

Numeric Field   A field that can contain only numeric data.

Option Group   A group of options that are related. Used to select a single option from a group of mutually exclusive options.

OR Operator   Used in a query to permit selection of records that meet one or another criteria, but not necessarily both.

Palette   A window displayed in the Form or Report Design View window. Used to add colors and special effects to selected objects.

Password   A unique series of characters assigned to a user allowing access to Microsoft Access.

Paste   The toolbar or menu command that copies the contents of the Windows Clipboard at the cursor's current location.

Permissions   The specific privileges assigned to a user that specify what parts of the database he or she can view, edit, or otherwise use.

Preview   A window that allows you to view forms and reports with actual data in them.

Que Cards   A special form of help that shows you how certain operations are performed.

Query   A question that you form on a Query Grid about the information contained in your database.

Query By Example (QBE)   The Microsoft Access method that you use to build your query question, by providing an example of the question that you want to ask.

Records   A complete collection of information represented by the fields of a single row in a table or form.

Report   Used to display selected information in an easy-to-read format. Reports can be printed or saved as a file.

Select Query   A query used to select and display specific records.

Sort Order   The order used to display your records. You can sort in either an ascending or descending order.

Table   A database object that displays information in a row and column format. Records are shown in rows and fields are contained in columns.

Text Box   A box that will accept any value that you type from your keyboard.

Text Field   A field that can contain any information entered by your keyboard.

Toggle Button   A control that you can use in a form that will enter a Yes/No or True/False type of response in a field.

Toolbar   The row of buttons displayed beneath the menu bar. The options available on the toolbar will vary depending upon your current actions.

Toolbox   A window containing a set of tools used in Design view of a form or report.

Undo   This toolbar or Edit menu option will undo the last change you have made to a field or record.

Wild-Card Character   Wild-card characters such as the asterisk *, question mark ?, number sign #, exclamation point !, hyphen -, and brackets [ ] are used to represent an unknown character(s), or patterns of characters in a query.

Wizards   A tool available to help you create certain types of tables, queries, forms, and reports.

Zoom   A button available on the Preview window toolbar, or whenever the mouse pointer appears as a magnifying glass. Zoom allows you to zoom in on a part of a page, or zoom out to a full page view.